Aikibatto
合気抜刀

Aikibatto
合気抜刀
Sword Exercises for Aikido Students

Stefan Stenudd

arriba.se

Stefan Stenudd is a 6 dan Aikikai Swedish aikido instructor, member of the Swedish Aikikai Grading Committee, President of the Swedish Budo & Martial Arts Federation, and Vice Chairman of the International Aikido Federation. He is also an author, artist, and historian of ideas. He has published a number of books in Sweden, both fiction and fact. Among the latter is an interpretation of the Chinese classic *Tao Te Ching*, and of the Japanese samurai classic *Go Rin no Sho* by Miyamoto Musashi. His novels explore existential subjects from stoneage drama to science fiction, but lately stay more and more focused on the present. He has also written some plays for the stage and the screen. As an historian of ideas he studies the thought patterns of creation myths, as well as Aristotle's *Poetics*. He has his own extensive website:
www.stenudd.com

Also by Stefan Stenudd:
Aikido Principles, 2008.
Attacks in Aikido, 2008.
Qi: Increase Your Life Energy, 2008.
Life Energy Encyclopedia, 2008, 2009.
Cosmos of the Ancients, 2007.
Your Health in Your Horoscope, 2009.
All's End, 2007.
Murder, 2006.

Cover: *Katana,* the Japanese sword. This blade is a work by the master smith Munetsugu, dated 1864, and made in Edo (present Tokyo), with a mounting of the *handachi* type. The length of the blade is about 74 centimeters. Munetsugu's swords were famous for their sharpness and functionality, and therefore highly appreciated by the Edo samurai. From the collection of Kjell Lindhberg. Photo by Ulf Lundquist.

Second edition.

Aikibatto: Sword Exercises for Aikido Students
Copyright © Stefan Stenudd 2007, 2009.
Book design by the author.
All rights reserved.
ISBN: 978-91-7894-023-3
Publisher: Arriba, Malmö Sweden, arriba.se

Contents

The author (to the left) shows a ken exercise at a Stockholm seminar in 2007. Uke is Mathias Hultman. Photo by Magnus Burman.

Foreword

Aikibatto is a system of sword exercises for aikido students. I developed it at my dojo Enighet in Malmö, Sweden, with the help of my aikido and iaido students. The kind and energetic assistance of Tomas Ohlsson was particularly valuable in the process.

I was also helped by the inspiring curiosity and cooperation of the members in dojos I visit regularly, such as Aikido Dojo Plzen, Tanden Aikido in Berlin, and the Lucenec and Martin dojos of the Slovak aikido organization SSPA. I have to mention my gratitude to Jaroslav Sip and Martin Svihla, who have done more than I would dream of asking from them.

The ten Aikibatto shoden exercises were presented on my website in June 2000, and the ten *jo* applications in May 2001. The ten okuden exercises are still to be completed, but I have not yet found an immediate need for them. The Japanese sword arts are all about the basics.

Malmö, September 2007
Stefan Stenudd

Osensei Morihei Ueshiba (1883-1969), the founder of aikido. Photo, courtesy of Yasuo Kobayashi.

Aikibatto

Background

In its usual curriculum, aikido contains a number of sword exercises and applications. These are not regulated by any Aikikai standard, since the Hombu dojo tends to exclude such practices from its schedule. Instead, prominent teachers usually have their own systems of practicing with the wooden sword, *bokken*, as well as with the staff, *jo*, such as the complex series of techniques developed by Saito sensei and Nishio sensei. Osensei Morihei Ueshiba, too, certainly practiced with the bokken and jo, as can be seen on the many films of him fortunately remaining.

Suburi is the basic training for achieving skills in handling the bokken. It usually contains solo exercises of cutting, thrusting, parrying and so forth. This type of training is necessary, if one is to learn an accomplished way of doing any swordplay with a partner. Also when it comes to partner exercises, it is necessary to find a basic system of techniques, where the suburi basics can be applied without too much complication, and where there is not too steep a ladder upward, from the reasonably simple techniques to the very advanced ones.

This is what I have tried to accomplish in this series of partner exercises with the sword: A system for learning the basics of the sword, in the spirit of *aikiken*, aikido swordplay, where one should be able to comfortably advance from the basic to the more complex techniques, yet always remain near the suburi forms of how to move the sword.

I also developed jo applications with the same intention. They are included in this book. Still, aikibatto is primarily a system of sword exercises, so the jo system should be regarded as little more than a complement.

Morihiro Saito (1928-2002), Aikikai 9 dan, showing one of his jo forms with Swedish aikido teacher Ulf Evenås. Photo by Jöran Fagerlund.

Aikiken and iaido

Aikiken is the term usually applied to bokken exercises in aikido. The word emphasizes that the techniques must be in accordance with the *aiki* principle of blending *ki*, the vital energy: the ki of the defender with that of the attacker. *Tori*, the defender, and *uke*, the attacker, should join.

On the surface, this is shown by the *taisabaki* moves out of the way of the attacking sword, as well as by the rhythm with which the counter moves are carried out. It also demands that the attacker's force is not stopped, nor his or her sword move blocked.

Iaido as it is normally practiced, for example in the standard form of *Seitei iai*, does not always apply the aiki principles in the way aikido does. Also, of course, iaido is practiced without a partner. Still, there are some immensely important things to be learned from iaido training, such as how the real blade behaves, compared to the wooden bokken, and what the rhythm is like in a series of moves, when the blows and the thrusts are carried through instead of stopped short, as they need be with a training partner.

Therefore, I strongly recommend that students practice both aikiken and iaido, preferably in a way that allows for a maximum of compatibility between the two. Thus, the best would be exactly the same series of techniques used in both aikiken and iaido. I have had this in mind when designing aikibatto, which can as readily be trained in solo kata style with a *iaito*, the sword for iai practice, or *shinken*, the sharp blade, as it can with a partner and the bokken.

My own sources are the aikido, aikiken, and iaido training I have done through the years. I started with aikido in 1972, when I was 18 years old. My first teacher was Allan Wahlberg, the head of that dojo. Soon, I also started training for Toshikazu Ichimura, who was at that time the national aikido teacher of Sweden. He was also 6 dan renshi in iaido, and held regular iaido classes in connection to the aikido classes.

Toshikazu Ichimura, aikido teacher in Sweden 1966-1986, leading a iaido class in the early 1970's. Photo by the author.

The teacher most inspirational to me must be Nishio sensei, who was a formidable authority on aikido, as well as on the sword and the jo. He developed an advanced system relating the aikido techniques to ken and jo. The first time I practiced for him was in 1981, and it was quite a bewildering experience. It took years just to see what he was doing.

Certainly, there are bits and pieces of his teachings in this system of aikibatto, but please rest assured that any mistakes or shortcomings in the techniques I have put together, have nothing to do with him. He would have been the first to correct them.

The website: aikibatto.com

Aikibatto has its own website at aikibatto.com, which you can also find a link to on my website stenudd.com. Most of the text and photos in this book, you also find on the website. Additionally, the website contains several video clips of the exercises.

You are free to any non-commercial use of everything on the website. If you copy parts of it to your own website, please include a link to the aikibatto website.

If you plan some use of the aikibatto website or of parts thereof, and you are not sure about your right to do so, please send me a request. You will find my contact information on the website, or you can use my email address: stefan@stenudd.com.

If I make changes on the aikibatto system of exercises, or additions to it, they will be posted on the aikibatto website. For example, when I finally get around to forming the ten *okuden* exercises, you will be able to find them there.

Shoji Nishio (1927-2005), Aikikai 8 dan, iaido 7 dan, judo 6 dan, kara-tedo 5 dan. Here he shows one of his ken forms at a seminar in the author's dojo Enighet, in Malmö, Sweden. Photo by Ulf Lundquist.

Aikibatto basics

Aikibatto, the name I have chosen for this system of exercises, is a combination of two concepts. *Aiki* is the joining of ki, which is so characteristic to aikido, and differs from the more head-on strategy common in iai and kenjutsu schools. *Batto* means drawing the sword or having drawn it, and was often used for the type of training today mostly called *iaido*. The word iaido means 'the way of joining with being'. It also implies sitting, since iaido usually includes seated forms.

I use the word batto, not particularly to connect to iaido, but to stress the fact that all these exercises start with *tori*, the defender, having the sword in the scabbard, or with the bokken in the belt. Thus, in every technique there must be a draw of the sword. Although this is very rare in aikiken training, I find it a pleasant statement of non-violence on behalf of tori, as well as a good exercise of timing and rhythm out of the unprepared state.

Shoden and okuden

Shoden and *okuden* are the two levels of teaching often utilized by traditional Japanese sword schools. Shoden, the first mediation, contains the basic techniques, suitable for the beginner, whereas okuden, the inner mediation, refers to what the advanced students are introduced to, when their level of understanding permits it.

The famous samurai Miyamoto Musashi sneered at such a division of a *ryu*. In his opinion the student must from the start learn only techniques which are functional all through – not something first, and later shift to something else. Certainly, one should never teach something that must be replaced later. There is only one thing, which takes more effort than teaching, and that is unteaching.

But if shoden is used for basics and okuden for the more complex techniques, and if both are available also to the beginning student (according to his or her ability), then there is some point to the division. That is how I have applied it, using the words shoden and okuden mainly to be in line with the traditional terminology, which is also good to learn.

Shoden

The ten exercises of shoden stress basic steps, turns, and sword moves. The link to iaido is particularly strong here, since every iaido school also has a number of *kata*, series of moves, presenting those basics. It is usually done in combinations of a few steps, mainly teaching the student how to draw the sword, *nukitsuke*, how to cut, *kiri*, and thrust, *tsuki*, and then how to shake off the blood, *chiburi*, finally to return the blade to the scabbard, *noto*.

For that reason, these moves are also included in aikibatto. Every exercise ends with tori doing noto, although with a bokken this may seem unnecessarily elaborate. If ex-

Miyamoto Musashi (c. 1584-1645), the famous samurai, in battle with Tsukahara Bokuden. Japanese woodprint, ukiyo-e, *by Yoshitoshi, 1885.*

cluded, though, one would still need to return the bokken to the belt before the next exercise. So, it makes more sense doing this in a proper way, similar to that used with a real sword.

Okuden

I have not yet completed the okuden aikibatto exercises, but here is what they are to contain:

The okuden sets are two, *nagare* and *taninzugake*, with five exercises in each. These terms are from aikido, not to my knowledge found in iaido. I use them for their obvious link to aikido training.

Nagare, flowing or streaming, means that the exercises should be performed in a non-stop, flowing style, preferably but not necessarily with a realistic speed. In aikido it's called *kinagare*, flowing ki. This usually means that uke attacks again and again, while tori moves continuously, never stopping on the spot.

In aikibatto I translate this to uke doing multiple attacks, while tori parries, counter attacks, parries again, in a series of techniques before the exercise stops. This is common in any aikiken system.

Training of this kind is not trustworthy without the student being properly trained also in suburi basics, as well as the more fundamental combinations of the shoden exercises. Otherwise, there is a strong possibility that the student will learn unfocused sword moves and imprecise steps.

Taninzugake is practice with several partners, multiple attackers, something which is very much kept alive in both aikido and iaido. I regard such training as essential in learning a sophisticated level of those martial arts, where the core of their strategies is revealed and put to the test.

Unfortunately, taninzugake is not practiced nearly enough in normal aikido training, as far as I have seen. But in iaido it is, through numerous kata where several attackers are assumed. When taninzugake is performed in aikido, usually only in dan examinations, it is more often than not solely the throw *kokyunage* against the attack *ryokatadori*, gripping both shoulders.

The aikibatto taninzugake exercises aim for a greater variety of techniques, both for the attacker and tori. They might help in adding comfort to a more varied training of taninzugake also in regular aikido.

Distance and contact

Regarding distance and contact, aikibatto is partly different from how many bokken systems operate. I think it is essential that the distance between tori and uke should be authentic, not extended so that they would actually not reach each other properly with the techniques.

This calls for additional precaution, to avoid accidents. But as long as that is understood, this way of training teaches accurate timing and movement.

The same goes for contact: When not causing damage, there should be some level of contact between tori's bokken and uke's body. Absolutely not on hard parts of uke's body, such as the head, ribs, or knees. But with caution it can be used for the soft parts, namely the waist and the wrists in most angles. This helps very much in learning the proper angle of the sword, and checking one's balance as well as the firmness of one's grip.

Contact should be carefully applied, so that there is no discomfort for uke. Also, one should take it as a reflex to check one's bokken for damages before exercising. Any unevenness on the bokken surface can hurt uke at the slightest contact. Such a bokken should not be used.

Equipment

Aikido students have their basic equipment, of course. For aikibatto, some additional things are needed – mainly a bokken, a jo, and a iaito or katana for those who want to be serious about the iai style training.

The aikido gear, called *keikogi* or *dogi*, consists of a jacket, pants, a belt, and a *hakama* for the advanced students.

Jacket

The jacket can be of either judo or karate type. Their main difference is the thickness of the cloth, where the judo jacket is the thickest. They also differ slightly in design. The judo style jacket is the most commonly used one in aikido, but there are many practitioners who prefer the karate jacket, because of its lightness. Myself, I mostly use the judo jacket, because of its design.

Whatever jacket you choose, I recommend that its cloth is not too thick – there are different levels of thickness also among judo jackets. It's not needed in aikido, where there is not at all as much pulling of the jacket as in judo.

Make sure that it is big enough, and remember that it might very well shrink a few percent when washed. The sleeves should not go all the way down to the hands, or all the wrist gripping in aikido gets complicated, but the jacket should be long enough to stay inside the belt even when you roll around on the mat.

Pants

As for the pants, they should not reach all the way down to your feet, but about halfway between the knees and the feet. I prefer those that are elastic at the waist, instead of being tied to place with a string, but the latter is probably the most lasting solution. Some extra fortification at the knees is good, so that the pants last for a lot of *suwariwaza* training.

The use of pants under the hakama is something particular to aikido. In kendo and iaido, for example, the practitioners have no other pants on than the hakama – well, underpants, surely. On the other hand, kendo and iaido allow the students to wear hakama from day one, whereas in aikido the students usually have to wait until they receive a certain grade, before they can put one on.

Belt

If you don't have a hakama, the belt, *obi*, you need to use is the same one as in judo and karate. You tie it with a knot below your navel. When you have a hakama, you can also decide to have another type of belt, the wide and thin one, *kaku obi*, which is usually much longer, and normally used with the traditional kimono. With this belt you should not make a knot below your navel. You can just stick in the end between some layers of it.

Hakama

Regarding the hakama, some prefer cotton – especially in kendo, since they have no pants under it, and cotton is pleasant against the skin. But I would say that artificial materials are more practical for aikido use. The hakama keeps its shape, and is easy to care for.

In aikido the hakama should be either black or dark blue, but in traditional iaido all kinds of colors and patterns are allowed – just as it was with this garment when the samurai used it. I remember that the former aikido *doshu*, Kisshomaru Ueshiba, used to wear a grey hakama on demonstrations, but present doshu Moriteru Ueshiba always wears a black one – at least so far. The kendo standard is

The author shows the angle of the feet at chudankame, *the middle level sword guard, at a seminar in Plzen, Czech Republic. Photo by Antonin Knizek.*

dark blue, because of their keikogi having the same color. There is one exception, though: Members of the Imperial dojo in Tokyo always wear a white hakama. It's just a tradition there, nothing they would themselves make any fuzz about. They probably regard it as rather impractical, since a white hakama is not easy to keep clean. Others should know this, if they wear a white hakama and keikogi: if you are not in the Imperial dojo – reconsider.

There are four straps on a hakama, two long ones at the front, and two shorter ones at the rear. Make sure that the straps are sturdy, and long enough to be tied properly around your body. There are so many ways to strap the hakama on. Aikido people often do it in elaborate ways, to make it stay in place through *ukemi* and *suwariwaza* training. The most accurately traditional way of strapping it on is done in iaido, but it is not ideal for severe aikido training. Ichimura sensei used to take it off after his iaido classes, and strap it on differently for his aikido classes.

Usually in aikido, you need to have received a certain

grade before you are allowed to put on a hakama. The most common grade for hakama is either 1 dan (for example in Japan), or 3 kyu (in most European dojos).

Some even have different demands for men and women, allowing the latter to put on the hakama at a lower grade. This is sometimes defended by the argument that the white *keikogi* pants are underpants, so women should be allowed to cover them with the hakama. If so, why not from the start – and why should men walk around in underpants? Strange. They are not underpants. In kendo and iaido they are simply not worn under the hakama, but underpants sure are. I find no reason at all for allowing women to put on the hakama at an earlier grade than men.

Actually, in the early days of aikido – before World War II – everyone was allowed, or even requested, to have a hakama from the first day of training. One of the Hombu dojo seniors, Okomura sensei, mentioned this in an interview. After the war, though, most Japanese were so poor that the dojo decided to allow beginner to wait until 1 dan, before getting a hakama – simply so that they were spared the expense for a while.

To my mind, there are only two complications in allowing beginners to wear a hakama: Firstly, they will have a more difficult time learning the basic movements, since moving in a hakama takes some getting used to. Secondly, other aikido students might expect them to be skilled at *ukemi*, the falling techniques, and throw them accordingly. Apart from the above, the students gain on putting on the hakama as soon as possible, since it helps them to cultivate the circular and sweeping aikido movements. Also, it stimulates them to root themselves steadily on the ground.

If you want to practice iaido, you really need a hakama to begin with. Without it, there is no practical way of making the bokken or sword stick inside your belt.

Bokken
Bokken, the wooden sword, exists in many shapes and materials. The former is more important than the latter.

In aikido there are two major kinds of bokken mostly used: One is curved and slim, much like a *katana*, an actual sword, the other is more sturdy and straight. The latter is used mainly by students of Morihiro Saito sensei's system, often referred to as *Iwama ryu* or *Takemusu*. Because of the kind of movements they do with the bokken – for example heavy *suburi*, and a lot of distinct contact between the bokken of the two players – they prefer this shape.

In iaido training, and in aikibatto, it is much better to use the curved and slim bokken. Its shape and balance is more near to that of the authentic sword, and the movements in both iaido and aikibatto are such that this shape leads to a better understanding of them.

The two most common materials used are called red oak and white oak. Usually, the latter costs a bit more, but that is not always the case. Also more exotic wood is used for bokken, but those cost a lot more. I had an ebony bokken once. It was a gift from a student. It was immensely more solid and strong than red or white oak ones, which seemed to soften at the mere presence of it. Well, it got stolen, and that is just as well. Several species of ebony are now endangered.

Try to get your bokken in a shop, where you can try it out, so that you are able to choose one with a nice balance, and a weight that you are comfortable with. Avoid a bokken that is significantly lighter than normal, because it is surely made of a material that is not solid enough. A bokken should feel compact. Also, make sure that it is not at all bent to the side.

Don't worry about the length of the bokken. The standard size will fit fine for anyone but extremely tall or short persons. Most bokken have the length of one meter or just above that. That is comparable to the sword length of 2.4 *shaku* (more about sword length below). I would say that if you are anything between 150 and 190 centimeters tall (5 to 6 feet), this bokken length will suit you fine. Otherwise, you may want to find a shorter or longer bokken – but that is not easy.

If you want to take proper care of your bokken, it should be oiled now and then. Use a fine grade sandpaper first, and then apply wood oil. Wipe off excess oil.

Jo

The staff, *jo*, has a standard length of 4.21 *shaku*, which is 127.5 centimeters (50 inches), and a diameter of around 25 millimeters (one inch). Like the bokken, it is mostly made of red oak or white oak.

The tricky thing with a jo is to get a straight one. When it is transported from one climate to another, it may twist slightly, and lose its straightness. I do recommend you to buy one in a shop, where you can roll it on a table or the floor, to check how straight it is. If you order one by mail, think twice before ordering the most expensive type.

Just as with the bokken, you need a solid material, hard enough to keep its shape, and not to break when you use it to ward off a bokken or another jo.

The length is a well established standard, so other lengths are not easy to come by. Like with the bokken, if you are somewhere between 150 and 190 centimeters (5 to 6 feet) tall, the standard length will be fine. If you are taller or shorter, you might want to consider a "tailor made" size of the jo. Either cut off a regular jo, to get a shorter size, or buy a *bo* (they are usually 6 shaku, which is circa 180 centimeters or 72 inches) and cut it down to your liking.

An old measure for the jo is to put it vertically on the ground. Then it should reach your armpit. That's longer than the standard 127.5 centimeters on most non-Japanese people, but don't be alarmed. Anything around the height of your nipples will do.

A too short jo might make you slide past the end of it when you extend it between your hands, which is a common movement in jo exercises. If you have that problem continuously, you may need a longer jo. And of course, if you have trouble comfortably reaching both ends of the jo, you surely need a shorter one.

As with the bokken, if you want to take proper care of

Jo against bokken. A movement in the seventh aikibatto jo exercise, kote chudan.

your jo, it should be oiled now and then. Use a fine grade sandpaper first, and then apply wood oil. Wipe off excess oil.

Iaito or shinken

If you want to train iaido or the iai form of aikibatto seriously, you need to get a sword. The bokken will do in the beginning, but it is with a sword that you can work on all the details. Only with a sword, you know what it is like to do the movements with one.

So, in iai style solo training, you might as well get a sword as soon as possible. Maybe after a month or so of getting used to the basic movements, by using a bokken.

There are so many sword shapes and qualities, but your major choice is between *iaito* and *shinken*. The former is an unsharpened, or semisharpened, sword made by alloys of zinc, aluminum, beryllium, or such, with a copper core. The latter is made of sharpened steel.

The iaito made of other metals than steel has been developed in Japan because of legal restrictions there. The only steel sword allowed to be made in Japan is the *katana* (or *tachi*) manufactured in the traditional way. Other swords may not be made in steel. Therefore, such production is done outside of Japan, often under Japanese supervision. Of course, the traditional katana is still made in Japan, by expert sword smiths.

If you prefer to start with a iaito, don't spend that much money on it. My guess is that after a few years you will want to shift to shinken. So, if you find a reasonably priced shinken, you might as well start with that – but use it with caution, because of its sharpness.

The Japanese sword is surrounded with myths about its formidable sharpness. It is impressive, but no magic. The sharpness of a well-made katana is comparable to that of a modern razorblade. Of course, a razorblade the length of two feet inspires some awe.

You can find lots of differently designed iaito, from about a couple of hundred US dollars up to above a thousand dollars. There's not much sense in paying that much for a iaito, though. Steel swords are made in China and other East Asian countries outside Japan, and costs from about 500 US dollars and up, up, up. In the lower price range, the blades are made in a semi-industrial way. Traditionally made katana – and antique ones – can be found from about 4,000 dollars, and good ones cost around 7,000. For, say, 15,000 dollars you can actually get a masterpiece made by a famous sword smith.

Whether you settle for a iaito or a shinken, I recommend you to keep it simple. No fancy decorations. Beauty is in its simplicity. And don't let elaborately made tsuba, tsuka, and saya, take your focus away from the blade. It's all about the blade.

Already with the blade, there are hundreds of different shapes. Well, surely thousands, upon closer examination. The curve of it can be steep or modest, but it should always form an elegantly curved line all the way from the tip of the blade through *tsuka*, the hilt. If you look at the sword from the side, this curved line should not be interrupted at the tsuba, or anywhere else.

Antique Japanese sword blades.

Antique Japanese swords with hamon, *the blade pattern.*

Aikibatto

Tomas Ohlsson, from the author's dojo, does noto, sheathing the sword. In iaido, a black jacket is common, but in aikido a white jacket is the standard.

Tsuba, the sword guard, is an art piece of its own, but for training purposes you should know that the weight of it does a lot to the balance of the sword. Normally, you would be better off with a tsuba that is not too thin and light, because you need the extra weight nearby the hilt, so that you can handle the sword smoothly. The most popular tsuba is one designed by the 17th century samurai Miyamoto Musashi, consisting of two thin oval rings. But that tsuba is very light, so it is not sure to give your sword the best balance.

I prefer a tsuba that is made of solid iron, and has the outer shape similar to a four-leaf clover. This gives a good place for the thumb to rest, away from the direction of the edge of the blade. Still, don't worry too much about it. Mostly you will do fine with whatever tsuba is already on the sword you buy.

Tsuka, the hilt, is usually covered with sharkskin, and cotton wrapped. Some are leather wrapped, and that is a good thing, guaranteed to last longer than the cotton, also giving better friction for the hands, so that your grip is more secure. The cotton wrapping works, too, but might be loosened or damaged after hours of practice.

Kashira, the end piece at the back of the tsuka, is usually either flat or rounded. I have found that the rounded type is more trustworthy, and more pleasant for the hand.

Mekugi is the little wooden pin that holds the blade to the hilt. It's an important little pin. If it breaks or pops up, there is a great risk that you send the blade flying when you swing the sword. So, check it frequently, and replace it if it gets very dry or broken. Some swords have two mekugi, but just one is far more common.

Saya is the scabbard. It is almost always a polished black, with no decorations. That's the best. You don't want your sword to be vulgar.

Sageo is the string by which you attach the scabbard to your belt. It is usually made by cotton or silk. You don't want it to be too thin, or it will quickly lose its shape and be difficult to tie properly. Stick with the color black, if that's what your saya is.

Again: avoid fancy colors and decorations. The traditional sword has no other colors on its details, than the black of the saya, the sageo, and the cotton wrapping of the tsuka, the off-white of the tsuka sharkskin, and so on. Remember that the real thing with the Japanese sword is the quality of the blade.

Another thing you need is the sword care set, by which

The *famous* tsuba, *sword guard, designed by the 17ᵗʰ century samurai Miyamoto Musashi.*

you keep the blade clean. If you have a iaito with an alloy blade, you don't have to be so careful with the cleaning, but a steel blade will start to rust if not properly cared.

You use *uchiko,* a powder of fine-ground polishing stone, to wipe the blade clean. Then you apply *choji,* a mineral oil with a minor addition of clove oil for flagrance, to protect it. The oil also makes the blade slide better in the saya, as well as on your hand in *noto.* Usually *nuguigami,* a special Japanese paper, is used for wiping the uchiko powder off the sword, but you can use other paper or cloth that does not scratch the blade's surface. You can also use certain other oils than choji – but why not stick to the real thing?

If you have a steel sword, especially if it is a traditionally made katana, you must clean it after every training. When it has been cleaned, make sure not to breathe on it, because of the water in you exhalation air. To be safe, make sure to clean it any time you have drawn the sword of out the scabbard, even if it was just to look at it.

The weight of a sword mainly depends on its length, but also on the exact shape of the blade. Normally a sword weighs about one kilogram (2.2 pounds) without the scabbard. A heavier sword is difficult to handle, and cutting many times with it is hard on your back and limbs. If you are not that strong or big, do not hesitate to get a lighter sword. You want to train iai for a lifetime, so there is no point in wearing yourself out in the first few years.

Regarding the length of the blade, westerners tend to exaggerate it, for the reason of us being significantly taller than most Japanese. But that quickly gets too far. Traditionally, the katana was not that very long at all, and a long blade is quite demanding to move in a katana way. If you are very tall, you may want a blade that is a couple of centimeters (up to one inch) longer than the standard, but don't take that for granted. Try a normal length out, before deciding on a significantly longer sword.

The blade length is measured as a straight line between the tip of the sword, and the *munemachi*, the point where it is covered by a collar usually made of brass. In Japanese tradition, a blade shorter than one shaku (30 centimeters, one foot) was a knife, *tanto*. A blade between one and two shaku (30-60 centimeters, 1-2 feet) was a *shoto*, for example a wakizashi or kodachi. A blade over two shaku (60 centimeters, 2 feet) was a *daito*, longsword, such as the katana and the tachi. Most katana blades were around 2.4 shaku (73 centimeters, 28.6 inches). That's a reasonable sword length, also for most westerners.

Shaku, sun, and bu

The traditional Japanese length measure is by *shaku, sun*, and *bu*. The shaku is about 30 centimeters (one foot), the sun is one tenth of that, and the bu is one tenth of a sun. So, writing a shaku measure by decimals is the same as writing it in shaku, sun, and bu. This is done with period marks: 2.4.5 stands for 2 shaku, 4 sun, and 5 bu, and it is the same as decimally 2.45 shaku.

Here is a table of measures:

1 *shaku*	=	30.3022 cm	=	11.93 inches
1 *sun*	=	3.03022 cm	=	1.193 inches
1 *bu*	=	0.303022 cm	=	0.1193 inches

Antique tsuba, *sword guards.*

Aikibatto

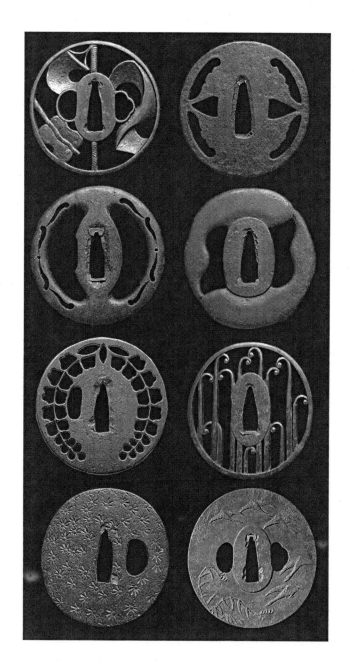

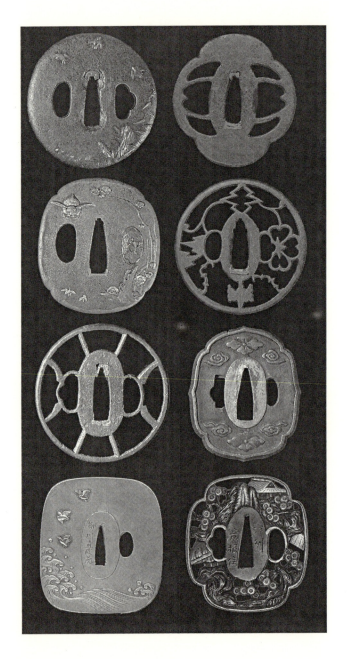

Reasons for aikibatto

The following three chapters were originally published in 2001 on the Iaido Journal at EJMAS.com, *Electronic Journals of Martial Arts and Sciences*, edited by Peter Boylan and Kim A. C. C. Taylor. The texts focus on the teaching and learning aspects of the aikibatto system.

Developing firm basics

This is how it started:

As a member of the Swedish aikido dan grading committee, I was looking at some of my own students being examined. I had to admit that when it got to their performance with the bokken and jo, they did not all of them do as well as could be expected. In our dojo we do a decent amount of training with those tools, and I would like to think that the instruction is not completely off the track. I had thought that my students should handle it well, also on a dan grading.

But they made their series of movements with some awkwardness, almost in a mood of alienation. They could grip their tools acceptably, and swing them too – but in the combination of movements there was a lot of hesitation, making it all less convincing.

Immediately I understood that they were not to blame, but I was. They were just expressing the backside of a teaching method I had been using for the last several years – one of improvisation, of always making up new combinations in class, not sticking to any system of exercises at all. Inventing kata as we went along.

Shoji Nishio shows a bokken technique at a 1990's seminar in the author's dojo Enighet. Photo by Ulf Lundquist.

Improvised budo

In aikido one would say that it was in a spirit of *takemusu*, improvised budo, born in the moment. I still believe that it is a mighty essence in any martial art – well, in any art.

I had hoped that by this my students would not only learn the applied basics of how to use the sword and the jo, but also make their minds free enough to choose techniques according to circumstance – instead of sort of freezing, when things did not go exactly according to plan. I wanted to teach them creativity, an open mind, and the ability that goes with it.

Instead, some of them – well, most of them - were uncertain about how to move from one position to the next, what action with which to meet the opponent's initiative, etcetera. They lacked firm understanding of how to apply their basic sword movements. Their improvisation became a random combination of techniques, sometimes in the right and functional places, sometimes not. Often they got completely lost in it.

It was clear that I had to rethink my teaching method.

From suburi to complexity

Myself, I have gone through a spectrum of teaching methods, through the years. When I started in the early 1970's, we had lots of hours with Ichimura sensei, where we were standing in a circle doing more *chudangiri*, cuts to middle level, than anyone could possibly enjoy. There was more to his teaching, of course, but the suburi, the repetitive exercising of basic movements, was always near at hand.

Almost ten years later we were introduced to Shoji Nishio sensei. Although Ichimura's teacher, he was a very different cup of tea. His movements were so complex and refined, it took us years – literally – just to perceive how he was moving. Not to mention how long it took to copy these moves, even in a very unpolished, clumsy way.

When struggling to learn Nishio sensei's way of using the sword and the jo, I was grateful to have been forced to do such a lot of suburi, long before, not having to think of that as well. It would have been too much.

I could see, though, that students who had not gone through a sufficient amount of basic training before trying to learn Nishio sensei's system, they had little chance of getting their basics right along the way. Quite the contrary. The many difficult and tricky moves seemed to seduce the students into ignoring the importance of basics – such as gripping, cutting, balance, center, and extension.

Anyone properly introduced into the sword arts would immediately say that without such basics, there is not much of a sword art remaining.

Actually, Nishio sensei also pointed this out. On one seminar, he suddenly interrupted the training of his complicated kata, to do some regular down to earth suburi. We did that basic training for a while, straightforward cutting exercises pretty much like in a normal kendo class. Then he explained to the congregation that this type of training must also be done.

It was for the local instructors to take care of, on a regular basis, so that when he came for a seminar, everyone could concentrate on what was more relevant for him to teach –

that is, the stuff even the local instructors were not properly competent with.

Breaking up in parts

With this in mind, I decided not to teach my students the full and exact system of Nishio sensei's ken and jo, but to break the kata up in small parts, do them in those small parts or mix them in different ways. This was to make my students focus on polishing the parts, instead of trying to rush through the complete combinations in a speed similar to that of Nishio sensei.

It worked rather well, I felt, especially in preparing the students for the Nishio sensei seminars. He visited our dojo several times during the 1990's. I could see that my students managed to perform the kata he showed us, although they had not learned the combinations by heart. But they were familiar with the parts. So, I still believe this is a good way of preparing students for Nishio sensei's system, if that is the goal.

On the other hand, this system of no system made my students lack in the ability to combine the parts convincingly. I realized that they were not enough familiarized with a way of doing so. Watching their efforts at that dan grading, I had to admit that some kind of system of exercises was needed.

Few movements, but all of them

Still, there was one thing to avoid: Too complex a system takes the student's mind off the basics, and a competent handling of the sword risks to be substituted with a vast number of kata, all of them poorly performed.

So, a system of basic sword training had to be simple – much like the *Seitei iai* of ZNKR (*Zen Nippon Kendo Renmei*, the Japanese Kendo Federation): a limited number of forms, with a very limited number of movements in each. Actually, this is pretty much like suburi in disguise. A way for the students to practice the basic movements repeatedly, without being too bored by it.

Yet, the system would have little meaning if it were not to include all of the important movements, and most of the others as well – at least the ones not regarded as odd or exotic in Japanese sword schools. It would be good, too, if a substantial part of sword art terminology is used, to be memorized and understood in its context.

Furthermore, being primarily aimed at aikido students, such a sword exercise system would need to fit reasonably well with aikido strategy, movements, and principles. For example, in many sword art techniques, the evasive step usually called *taisabaki* in aikido, is absent. Instead, there is often a head-on movement of the body. Not so in for example Nishio sensei's iaido system (he called it *Aikido Toho*), but certainly in the Seitei iai of ZNKR. If not, the latter would probably do fine as a system of basic sword exercises also for aikido students.

There is one more ingredient needed for the aikidoka: the partner training, the fencing if you will. Seitei iai could probably be trained in such a way, if some creative thinking is applied to it, but not ideally – especially not for aikidoka.

I needed a basic system, then, possible to train – without changing its forms - solo in iaido fashion, or with partner. That was to be aikibatto.

A sword for the aikidoka

So, what is needed of a sword exercise system? The question cannot be answered without first deciding what should be learned from it. A basic understanding of the traditional Japanese sword arts is a self-evident first. But for me as an aikido teacher, I would have to add that this understanding and its applications should be in the framework of aikido's principles and strategy.

A sword art, then, for the aikidoka.

That is a risky business indeed. When trying to apply the sword to aikido concepts, one might easily happen to substitute the functional with something else, which might look good and feel fine, but lacks essentials for the sword to be handled according to its own terms. Those terms are in some cases just as sharp as the sword's edge.

One needs to be systematic, especially in deciding what should be learned. When I constructed the aikibatto exercise system, I found it helpful to think along two lines of demands: those of the sword arts, and those of aikido.

Sword art demands

The sword art related demands I would like to see as *suburi* needs on one hand, and a general understanding of sword strategy on the other. Suburi includes such fundamentals as posture, how to grip the sword, and of course how to cut with it. Those are elements that take a lifetime, nothing less, to adapt properly.

Having practiced with the sword for more than a third of a century, I still experience new revelations now and then, when it comes to gripping the sword, or raising it to *jodan-kamae*, not to mention doing a cut, a thrust, a parry. Nothing but practice, year after year, can bring refinement in these details.

But this practice, with repetition and a certain monotony being essential to it, still has to be done in a spirit of curiosity, inspiration, delight – or little will be learned from it. I don't believe suburi is doing its job optimally, when the students find it boring. So, I knew I would have to make suburi a substantial part of the exercise system, but disguise it, not to strike the students as terribly predictable, and dull like household chores.

Regarding the strategy of the sword, I simply refer to such things as rhythm or timing, how to move the sword from one position to the next, how to meet different attacks, how to position oneself in relation to the opponent, etcetera. This cannot be completely understood in solo kata practice alone. One has to try it out with a partner.

Still, the solo exercise is necessary as well. Without it, the students will have great difficulties in experiencing the demands of the sword itself – how it can be moved swiftly, and how not, how to cut with it, and how not to cut oneself

Tomas Ohlsson makes the draw in ukenagashi, *the third form of Seitei iai, the iaido of Zen Nippon Kendo Renmei.*

in the process. Mainly, the solo *kata* training establishes the necessary link, one might even call it bondage, between the student and the sword. They should act as one. Without solo training, I do not think it can be accomplished.

So, the sword art aspects demanded of my exercise system to contain a lot of suburi, but disguising it in different combinations of movement, and to be trained both solo and with a partner.

Aikido demands

In aikido the partner exercises are central. Solo training is both rare and peripheral. So, a sword system without partner training would be alienating to the aikidoka. A *tori* and *uke* exchange is the path, the source, and the solution. Two centers interacting, to the point of becoming one.

Nevertheless, at the outset there are two centers, which should be clearly defined. In the partner training of aikido, this is sometimes neglected. The two intermingle and adapt to each other, until there is no longer a difference between tori and uke. That is a situation of quite some philosophical beauty, no doubt, but if not reached the long way, I do not believe it speaks true *budo*.

So, also the aikidoka needs some aspects of training that have a clear solo exercise ingredient. The sword art is evidently very suitable for this.

Still, if the strategy of aikido is to be respected, the movements have to be constructed in such a way that they conform to this particular strategy. Allow me to pinpoint the most essential elements of it, which seem to be suitable to express in the negative: No attack but only defense, no resisting or blocking of attacks, no need of superior force, no halting of the flow of the movement. Much of this is incorporated in other martial arts as well, but the aikido strategy has an uncompromising focus on it.

Four negatives needed

'No attack' means waiting for the opponent to charge, before taking any action. In aikibatto (as in iaido) this is stressed by tori starting with the sword still in the scabbard, not drawing it until the attack commences. The more common starting position in aikiken (and kendo), that of *chudankamae* against the same guard, is not the optimal aikido attitude. It also creates the strategic problem of uke not being able to withdraw from *kamae*, without feeling a risk of easily being struck by tori. Uke is sort of blackmailed into attacking. For tori to be in no way attacking, means a starting position where the sword is not drawn.

'No resisting' means stepping out of the way of the attack, so that it can be completed – without the defender being hit by it. In aikido, this is done by the *taisabaki* body move, usually forward to the side of uke. For suburi purposes, this also has the advantage of uke not having to stop the cutting move prematurely. In aikibatto, uke is mostly exercising little else than the straight cut, the fundament of the sword arts.

'No superior force' means that the counter moves should be done in openings caused by the original attack, and not by maneuvers which demand of tori to have superior speed or power.

In budo it is discovered that the attacker cannot avoid creating openings for the defender to exploit – that is, if the initial attack was not successful. This pacifying circumstance is just as true also in a second or third attack, wherefore I did not introduce any additional exchange of charges in the shoden exercises of aikibatto. No tori blows are blocked or otherwise avoided by uke. That would have dimmed the understanding of this rhythm – the shortcut available to the one not attacking. That is also why all the counter techniques are done either at the same time as the attacks, or immediately following them.

In the so called *okuden* set of exercises, though, I plan to include some fencing, where both tori and uke have their strikes avoided by the opponent.

'No halting of the flow' means that the counter moves should be performed so that they do not stop the attack but rather complete it, or make the attacker continue in the direction initiated by his or her attack. Thereby, uke is able to exercise proper attacking techniques fully. But more importantly, this is a sort of economy of battle, which is central to aikido thinking. Few things are of such help in getting an advantage in the duel, as the ability to extend the attacker's moves beyond their initial aim – causing uke to lose both time and balance. But as Musashi would have put it: That takes a lot of training to accomplish.

Basic bokken training. Chudankamae, middle guard. From a 2005 seminar in Lucenec, Slovakia. Uke is Martin Frankovic.

The teacher is the needle

Below, I hope to be able to explain my reasons behind making the ten exercises of the shoden set in aikibatto. This takes me into some detail of each of the exercises, so you may want to get familiar with them before reading this.

To start by summing it up: It's all a matter of teaching. I am reminded of Musashi's words in *Go Rin no Sho*, The Book of Five Rings: The teacher is the needle, the student is the thread. To teach, you must be bold and go ahead – but when the work is done, the students remain, holding it all together, while the teacher has no function anymore.

I needed a system, for my aikido students to practice and understand some of the sword art basics. Therefore, you will find that my reasons for putting together the exercises as I did, always boil down to pedagogics.

Still, there are also choices made from my understanding of the martial arts and their perspectives. I have allowed myself to construct the aikibatto in accordance with what I personally find to be the most sound, the most convincing and trustworthy. Others may make other choices, and surely have good reasons for them. Truth is a process.

Here is how I have reasoned:

Why ten?

The first that comes to an inquisitive mind, is why I have made ten exercises – not, say, six or eighteen. Actually, in the process of creating them, that decision came last. I simply put together exercises, one after the other, until I felt that I had included the techniques and combinations called for in a basic shoden set. They happened to be ten.

Well, I wanted to keep the number down, so it was unlikely that I would allow for that many more than ten.

I would not have objected to fitting everything into just six or so. But that was impossible, if not allowing each exercise to be a series of attacks and defenses, like regular fencing. This I did not allow. Each exercise had to be short, little more than one attack and a decisive defense on it.

Wham bam...

In a basic understanding of the Japanese sword arts, it must be realized that it is unlikely with a lot of exchange of blows, like in movies about Sir Lancelot and the like. In principle, and I would guess in historic reality, it is more of a wham, bam. The first attack, if succeeding, immediately ends the duel. If failing, the duel is ended by the counter attack. That's it.

It is in the nature of the katana – its sharpness, and the way it is handled. Also, it is an important principle of budo: the now, and not the next.

So I made the shoden exercises very short. In the coming okuden sets, though, I plan to allow for more prolonged exchanges between *tori* and *uke*, the defender and the attacker.

Everything in pairs

Early in the process of creating the exercises, I found out that it would be very reasonable to divide them into pairs. It has two advantages: One is that you then explore a certain aspect from two angles. The other is that the full set is easier to remember for the students, as they can group the exercises - a bit like rhymes in lyrics.

Maybe it also helps introducing the students to an *in-yo* (yin-yang) way of thinking, which is central to all East Asian philosophy. The two sides of things, the opposites uniting, and so forth. This is also evident in budo terminology, which very often has a pair of terms, opposites, needing to be considered. It is especially present in aikido, with its *omote-ura*, *irimi-tenkan*, and so forth.

In another dimension of the twine, how natural is it not for the student to ask, after trying out an exercise: "But what if..." The pairs may not be universal and reciprocal answers to any what-if, but they stimulate the students to find out for themselves.

The pairs of aikibatto exercises are presented in this table:

Aikibatto shoden

SHIHO four directions

1	*MAE front*	2	*USHIRO back*
3	*HIDARI left*	4	*MIGI right*

UKENAGASHI parry

5	*OMOTE straight*	6	*URA reverse*

KOTE wrist

7	*CHUDAN middle*	8	*JODAN high*

HARAI ward off

9	*ATE strike*	10	*TSUKI thrust*

First a foursome

I have to start by sort of breaking the rule explained above. The first exercises are actually a foursome – the four directions of front, back, left, and right. Still, they could be paired: front and back, left and right.

I present them as a foursome – *shiho*, four directions – because this is basic budo. The idea of those four directions is of almost cosmological significance, not only in East Asian thinking. A budoka not practicing the four directions, risks becoming far too narrowminded, locked to prerequisites that may not always be the case.

So, I constructed the first four exercises as sort of one and the same, only changing to the minimal extent needed because the attacker comes from different directions. It is important for the student to see that a good movement should be applicable to several situations, not just one – but also that any movement, no matter how clever, needs some adaption to specific circumstances. In other words: open mind.

The ukenagashi pair

Next is a pair of *ukenagashi* exercises. The ukenagashi is a very essential and basic sword movement, warding off the attack at the same time as entering close enough to strike. In

Bokken practice with four attackers, on a 2006 seminar in Plzen, Czech republic. Photo by Antonin Knizek.

the Japanese sword arts, ukenagashi is one of the most important movements, so it should be exercised early and repeatedly. It is a very effective and trustworthy technique, when properly done.

In this pair the cut is not straight, but a diagonal one, *kesagiri*. This cut was far more common in samurai times, because it avoided such hard targets as the helmet and the spine vertically. Also, it is a more adaptive way of cutting, applying to many more situations.

There is a rude joke in its name. *Kesa* are the suspenders worn by zen monks. The cut follows these diagonal lines on the body. Let's hope that it was not practiced on the monks, though.

The ukenagashi parry almost automatically leads to the kesagiri cut, which is why they are combined in the aikibatto exercises. The push that uke's sword gives tori's sword, becomes the start of the kesagiri cut. Therefore, it can be done extremely fast, so it is next to impossible for uke to counter.

The pair of ukenagashi exercises consists of *omote* and

ura, quite familiar to aikido students. Most aikido techniques exist in these two forms. But omote and ura are well-known concepts also in Japanese society outside of aikido.

Omote means outside, front, surface. The kanji for it signifies originally the hairy side of the fur, i.e. its outer side. Symbolically, it could be compared to the concept of face value, what is obvious and clear.

Ura means reverse side, backside, inside, the hidden, the inner. Its kanji relates to the inside of the fur, or the lining of a garment. The word is used for things hidden, what lies behind what seems to be.

In aikido the symbolic values of the two are rarely stressed, although that could be rewarding for the aikido student to consider. Instead, omote is basically entering to the front of uke, whereas ura techniques include a turn behind uke.

That is also the case in the aikibatto applications. Omote is a straightforward counter movement, where ukenagashi is swiftly followed by keasgiri. Very wham, bam. In ura, uke has time for a second strike, so tori moves to the other side of uke – not really behind him or her, but almost so.

Sword applications of omote and ura are essential to aikido students, in order to understand their significance, and to be able to adapt them to circumstance.

The kote pair

Kote is the wrist. In kendo the word is used for the wrist protection, that is the collar of the thick glove worn in kendo. Different kanji are used for the wrist and its kendo protection.

In aikido, kote refers to the wrist, since it is the actual wrist that is manipulated in such techniques as *kotegaeshi, nikyo,* and *sankyo.* Therefore, I use that kanji also for the aikibatto kote techniques, although that is not usually the case in the sword arts.

Wrist manipulation is an important part of aikido, and striking the wrist is just as important in the sword arts. The major reason for the latter is that the attacker's wrist is usually much easier to reach than his or her body, and striking at the wrist will surely make the attacker unable to move the sword sufficiently.

The relation between the kote sword strike and the many wrist techniques in aikido is indeed interesting. It should be explored.

The kote pair in aikibatto is *chudan* and *jodan*, middle and high level. There are actually three levels in budo, the third of them *gedan*, low level. But neither in aikido nor in the Japanese sword arts is the gedan level used that much, so it is not necessary to cover in the shoden set of aikibatto exercises.

Chudan, the middle level, is at belly height. The most important example of it is in *chudankamae*, the middle level guard, where the sword is held in front of one's center, *tanden*. Musashi called this the field marshal of guards, stressing its sovereignty over the other guards. It is like a closed fortress. If you have a solid and living chudankamae, it is very difficult for the opponent to find an opening for a strike. It should be practiced as solemnly as one meditates, and with a similar spirit.

The basic chudan strike is *do*, the kendo strike at the belly protection with the same name. You can also call it *yokogiri*, a sideways cut. This is a very effective technique in kendo, although not used that very much – mainly because the referees tend to ignore it, don't ask me why. In the aikibatto exercise, it's not the belly but the wrist that is the target. This is a very common attack in kendo, and the referees certainly don't ignore it.

Jodan, the high level, refers to head height or above it. Its guard is *jodankamae*, where the sword is held above the head. This guard makes striking very quick and easy, but the body is not as protected as in chudankamae.

The basic jodan attack is *men*, to the head. Both *shomen*, the straight cut to the head, and *yokomen*, the side cut. Both are very common in the Japanese sword arts. In this aikibatto exercise, the latter is used – as well as a kote cut at the high level.

Aikido revolves around the center – that of uke and that of tori alike. Therefore, aikido students tend to get more familiar with chudan than with jodan, whether in attack or in defense. I would agree that in aikido – in a way also in the sword arts – chudan is of greater importance than jodan. But that should be learned from experience. There is no point in neglecting jodan. That can only lead to flawed and incomplete budo. It should also be remembered that people tend to relate to each other on jodan level – through their faces rather than their bellies. That is also true for many martial arts.

So, one should remain in one's center, but with a jodan awareness. Hopefully, this is encouraged by the two aikibatto exercises.

Notice also that these two exercises introduce a new attack form for uke. Instead of the chudankamae start of all the previous exercises, uke starts with *miginowaki*, the right side guard, which leads to a mighty forward swing of the sword. It is simply time for uke to train another attack, after having been drilled sufficiently with the basic forward cut from chudankamae. Still, the persistence with the basic attack through all the previous six exercises gives it the dominant position needed.

The harai pair
In this pair of exercises, uke gets to do a different technique: the *tsuki* attack, the forward thrust of the sword.

This attack is good for aikido people to experience as tori, since it demands another distance and timing than what is often used in aikido training. In *tachidori*, defense against sword attacks, many aikido students practice almost exclusively *chudangiri*, a straight cut to middle level. Therefore, they often allow themselves to begin at a distance, *maai*, which is so close that uke can actually reach them with a quick tsuki. When you practice defense against tsuki sufficiently, you are less likely to make that mistake.

Of course, it is also good for uke to exercise this very basic attack form in the sword arts. In kendo, it is only done as *jodantsuki*, aiming at the opponent's throat, where there is a special protection against it. In iaido, both jodantsuki and *chudantsuki*, to the opponent's body, are used. The chudantsuki is usually done toward solar plexus, but with the blade turned sideways it could also go for the heart.

Harai, sometimes pronounced barai, is a warding off movement that can be done with the blade, the hilt, or even the saya. In both the aikibatto exercises it is done with *tsuka*, the hilt, before tori's sword is drawn. This is particularly interesting for the aikido student, since it is done with the same distance and timing as should be used in unarmed defense. The way the warding off is done could be performed with a bare hand as well – or even more practically with the lower arm.

The first harai exercise follows up with *ate*, a strike. This is a familiar technique in aikido, where it's called *atemi*, which means strike to the body. It is mostly done by an unarmed hand, and used to distract the attacker, rather than to actually hit him or her. In the sword arts, though, a real strike is intended.

Ate in the sword arts is done with *tsuka*, the hilt – to be more precise, its end piece, *kashira*. This part of the sword is made of metal, so it is hard enough. Usually, the strike is done with the sword still in the saya.

Again, this teaches the aikido student the same distance and timing as should be used in unarmed atemi. A good aim is also necessary, to make the technique effective. Such a strike has little effect on some parts of the body, and more on others. In the aikibatto exercise, the aim is solar plexus. The throat is another common target for ate in the sword arts.

The second harai exercise follows up with *chudantsuki*, a thrust with the sword on middle level, toward the attacker's solar plexus. In paired training, though, tori should intentionally aim the thrust beside uke's body, to be able to extend the technique without hurting uke. The timing with which the tsuki is to be done, is such that uke sort of rushes right into it. That is an interesting timing to work with, also in many aikido techniques.

The actual tsuki is rather short, just enough to penetrate the attacker's body completely. It is followed up with a prolonged tsuki movement, which is actually to push the attacker off the blade. This is included to remind the students of sword arts that one has to think about what happens to the sword, when a strike is completed. The blade is stuck deep in the attacker's body. So, it cannot be swung freely right after the strike. First, it has to be removed from the attacker's body.

I have seen many iaido forms, where the sword is lifted right up after chudantsuki, although that would mean lifting a whole body still attached to the sword. Think about it. You would have to be extremely strong to do that, if it is at all possible.

So, though it is kind of a gory thing, if you think about it, I have included this example in aikibatto. You need to think about how to get the sword out of the attacker, after your strike.

The other aikibatto exercises are designed with this in mind, but it is not as obvious in them.

Nuke – drawing the sword

Batto simply means drawing the sword. Another word often used in iaido is *nukitsuke*, which implies drawing the sword and striking with it in the same movement. The first half of that word, pronounced *nuke*, is the draw itself.

In the sword arts, there are not so many different ways to draw the sword. It has to come out of the saya, so the direction is given. Differences in draws have to do with how the sword is gripped, and what movements precede and follow it.

In the aikibatto shoden series, the first four exercises have nukitsuke, the draw and strike in one movement, which is very basic in all iaido. The same is true for the two *kote* exercises, although the strikes differ. In the fifth and sixth exercise, the draw is to a parry, and in the last two exercises, the draw follows after *ate* or *harai* done with *tsuka*, he hilt.

Nukitsuke, *the draw and strike of the sword, at a 2002 Plzen seminar. Photo by Larry Kwolek.*

Other ways of drawing are possible, of course, but not basic enough to be included in the shoden set. I will include some of them in the okuden set.

Chiburi and noto

Chiburi is shaking off the blood from the blade, after the attacker has been struck down. It is done at the end of every iaido kata, also each of the aikibatto exercises.

There are several different ways of doing this. None is really so efficient that the blade would be clean enough to return to the scabbard, without additional cleaning. The blade would still be stained, and start to rust in no time. In old times, the additional cleaning was done with a cloth. That is excluded from iaido, probably in order for the training not to be too gory, or just to save some time.

The aikibatto shoden exercises include five different chiburi. That's actually all I know, and all I have seen so far. They are included, so that the students can get familiar with them.

I have given them Japanese names that are not traditional, but hopefully logical and easy to remember for aikido students:

Chiburi	Exercise
Chudan, middle level	*1, 2*
Gedan, low level	*3, 4*
Migi, to the right	*5, 6*
Jodan, high level	*7, 8*
Kaiten, rotation	*9, 10*

As you can see, the chiburi are in the same pairs as the exercises are arranged in whole. That should make it easy to remember which chiburi goes where, but the reason is another: I find that a certain chiburi comes naturally from what position you are in at the end of the exercise, after your last strike. So I paired the chiburi with the exercises accordingly.

In the first two exercises, you end with the sword at chudankamae, so it makes sense to make the chiburi on that level. In the next two exercises you end with the sword at gedan level. This chiburi and noto I learned from Nishio sensei, and I have not seen it elsewhere. In the fifth and sixth exercise you end with the sword in an angle that invites a chiburi to the right. In the seventh and eighth exercise you end with a *yokomen* strike, so your sword is at jodan level. In the last two exercises the sword ends at chudan level, so you could do the same chiburi as in the first two, but also the rotation chiburi – and the latter feels more natural to me after *chudantsuki*, the thrust to middle level.

Noto is to put the sword back in *saya*, the scabbard. This is connected to what chiburi you do. The chiburi and noto should be seen as a whole.

I should point out that in the rotating chiburi, I follow Nishio sensei's way of doing noto, which differs from how it is done in some sword schools. That is because I find it much more controlled and safe than other ways I have seen. One should not have as a habit to take unnecessary risks at getting hurt by one's own sword.

Now, it is time for me to explain what intentions I had with each separate exercise in the aikibatto system.

1 Mae

The first exercise must be a *mae*. To me, that is obvious. Mae is not only a simple way of dealing with a straight attack from the front, but a sort of declaration of content for the whole sword school, or in this case the whole series of exercises. So much is stated  about strategy, principles, attitude. It can be compared with the opening scenes of a movie. Just about everything has to be told.

So, in the aikibatto mae, some choices are presented. For example, it does not start in *seiza*, sitting. I prefer to postpone that to the okuden set, simply because the sword arts firstly and naturally relate to standing up, and walking about. In many iaido schools, I think there's far too much sitting down. With the *katana*, the normal longsword, this makes little sense. With the shorter *wakizashi* or *tanto*, the knife, it would be more understandable. Historically, the samurai never had the katana stuck in the belt when seated.

Well, in aikido there is a big curriculum of *suwariwaza*, training on one's knees. It is a fine physical exercise – if you have good knees when you start to train it. It teaches balance, economy of movement, and much more. Still, is it good enough to be done close to half of the time, as it is in some iaido schools, already for the beginner? I doubt it.

That's a choice of mine, certainly controversial to many.

Furthermore, in mae the defender starts with the sword in the scabbard. This is normal in iai, of course, but rare in *aikiken*, aikido sword exercises. Anything else would be less of an introduction to the sword arts, but more importantly: it would be aggression. If both have their swords drawn at the beginning, what is to say that one is an attacker and the other not?

Also, I salute the principle of the *kamae*, guard, which is no kamae. The defender should start from a position seemingly unready, thereby learning always to be ready without having to show it. One cannot live one's whole life with one's sword drawn (also in a metaphorical sense).

Next, mae shows the strategic basics: not stopping or blocking the attack, but using it with a timing that is simultaneous and ends the duel right after the attacking blow is completed: *ta-da*.

Once this is established in the first exercise, it is permissible to make small deviations from it in the following.

Much more is stated in the "opening scene" of mae, such as how to move one's sword as well as one's body, but I do not think these kinds of aspects are much different in aikibatto from sword arts in general.

2   Ushiro

After so many words on mae, I don't think too much needs to be added about *ushiro*, where the attack is from behind. One thing, though: Regarding the timing, I did not want to demand too much of speedy action from the one who is surprise attacked from behind. A move to the side to avoid the cut, nothing more, initially. That's enough to hope for, in a situation of that kind.

This moving away, though, is a valuable technique in itself, deserving to be exercised. I tell my students that they should think of it as a reflex movement, when sensing the attack from behind – hearing it, getting a glimpse of it, or even actually sensing it without perceiving it. But when training it, I ask of them to turn their heads and look at the attacker from the beginning. This is to avoid accidents, and to keep the students confident.

I actually believe that this sort of training – in spite of the precaution of looking back from the start – heightens the awareness to a point where chances are increased that an attack can be sensed, before physical evidence of it is perceived. I jokingly say that this takes some time, hinting that I mean a very long time indeed. But my personal experience is that this instinct, if that is the word, really comes quickly.

I had some convincing experiences along this line, only a few months after I started practicing aikido. Of course, that was in my teens – a time of life when one is quite receptive.

Just like mae, ushiro stresses the importance of commencing with grabbing one's sword and drawing it – before even knowing what's going on. That too, is good to rub in.

3   Hidari

In most cases, in budo and elsewhere, the order of the directions is such that right comes before left. The reason I have for switching it in aikibatto, is that left, *hidari*, is done pretty much like mae and ushiro, while right, *migi*, introduces some significant changes in the movements.

With the pair of left and right, I see the attack coming from around the corner of a building, or some other obstacle. Therefore, the attacker is invisible beforehand, hidden behind the wall. If this were not the case, there would not be much point in practicing left and right attacks particularly. When the attacker is spotted before charging, the situation will turn into mae. Who does not face an adversary straight on, when given the opportunity to do so?

For the hidari exercise, this does not make much difference, except the importance of understanding the timing for both attacker and defender. The attacker, hiding behind a wall, also cannot see the other person beforehand, and is therefore unable to charge before the defender appears from behind the wall. That gives the defender a chance to react.

Another interesting thing to be aware of, is that the attacker cannot stand too close to the corner, at least not with a *chudankamae*, the middle level guard. Otherwise, the defender would spot the sword and be warned – before the attacker sees the defender! So, the attacker has to stand a few

Yokogiri, *or* do, *the horizontal cut. From a 2002 seminar in Jönköping, Sweden. Uke is Stefan Jansson, of the Brandbergen Aikido dojo.*

steps back from the corner, which again gives the defender some additional chance to react.

If the attacker were to stand in *jodankamae*, the guard with the sword above one's head, the position could be closer to the corner. In such a situation, I wonder if there is much chance for the defender to avoid the attack at all. Certainly, it is not a shoden thing. So I stick to chudankamae, and the distance called for.

Let's say that even a lurking attacker feels safer with the chudankamae than with the jodankamae. In the case of the latter, tori has to have an awareness allowing for either an immediate retreat, or a just as immediate advance past the aim of uke's cut. But again, this is beyond shoden.

In the first two shiho exercises, the defender ends with a *chudan* cut, down to middle level, but in hidari and migi it is *gedan*, to low level. The first is the most basic, fundamental to the Japanese sword arts, but the gedan cut is a very good way of learning to relax one's shoulders in cutting, and therefore helps to improve the cutting.

Also, it is a basic cut, needing to be included in an exercise system. And it is a practical cut, since it goes all through the opponent's body, instead of getting stuck in the middle of it. Therefore, in *taninzugake*, against several opponents, it is to prefer.

The *chiburi* and *noto* , the shaking off the blood and the sheathing of the sword, also differ from the first two exercises. I intended to let the students try out several different chiburi and noto, just to widen their experience – and to have some fun. I have tried to link each chiburi to the exercise where it seems the most appropriate, the most fitting, and with the same logics the noto following depends on what chiburi is used.

I learned this particular chiburi and noto from Nishio sensei. I have not seen it elsewhere.

4   Migi

This is kind of fun: When tori is attacked from the right side, the response needs to be quite different from in the previous three exercises. The reason is an obvious one, if we picture a  situation where the attacker waits around the corner of a building. Trying to move away from the attack to the right, like in the earlier exercises, would mean stepping right into the wall. Not very practical.

In some other sword art solutions to a migi attack, this is not considered, but to me it seems like an interesting aspect to work on. So, in the aikibatto form of migi, the movements are consequences of the attacker's left side not being accessible. Instead, the defender moves to the right side of the attacker, adjusting *yokogiri*, the side cut, accordingly.

Also in the draw to *jodankamae*, the wall on the defender's right side must be considered. There is not room for a horizontal sweep to the right, as in previous exercises. Instead, the sword is spun around vertically.

In all the four exercises of the shiho set, a straight cut is used at the end, and not a diagonal one. There are two reasons for this:

One is the simple fact that the straight cut is the most basic, needing the most training, which is why it is also the most frequent technique used by the attacker. The other reason is more so to speak surgical: A straight cut is not very practical on a person standing straight – there is too much hard stuff to cut through. But after having been hit with the yokogiri, the attacker is most likely to bend forward, so that the straight cut does in effect strike as a *kesagiri*, diagonal cut, would.

I beg your pardon for this rather nasty aspect of it, but some such things also need to be contemplated, in order to understand the sword arts.

5   Omote

Now, we leave the four directions to focus on an attack from the front in all the remaining exercises. This makes sense to me, since an attack from any direction is quickly turned into a *mae* situation if the defender has time to turn toward it – and that should have been learned by the previous foursome.

The following pair is a study of the *ukenagashi* warding off of the attacker's sword – a technique of vast importance in the sword arts, and also in martial arts without any weapons. In one or other variation, it exists in aikido as well as karatedo, and I find it ever so useful in numerous situations.

This should be understood: In the sword arts, ukenagashi is not primarily a parry, but a way of drawing the sword to *jodankamae*, having also the additional benefit of being a good parry. But the best way to avoid a sword attack is to move away from it. Rarely is it trustworthy to stand one's ground and try to block or ward off a blade swung in one's direction.

Step away! And draw the sword simultaneously. To me, that's optimal.

The ukenagashi position of the sword should be such that it can be immediately followed by a cut. No additional adjustment of the sword position should be needed before the cut. The rhythm of *ta-da*.

Omote is an exercise of this very basic *ta-da*: Draw the sword in an ukenagashi move, then cut immediately. In this case – as opposed to the previous exercises – the attacker is still standing straight, wherefore a *kesagiri* diagonal cut is used instead of a straight one. This also comes naturally after the ukenagashi move.

It is possible to do this movement very quickly – or the attacker would have time to parry, or draw for a new cut.

6   Ura

In the ura, on the other hand, we presume that the attacker is fast enough to have time to draw for a new cut, before a kesagiri can be executed. To make this more likely – and to prepare the student for alternative movements of the attacker – this attack is *men*, to the head, and not a cut all the way down to *chudan* level. From a men cut, the next strike comes very quickly indeed, for someone well trained with the sword.

This second cut of the attacker will not be in the same direction as the first one, but to the left (seen from the attacker), since that is the new position of the defender. This is important to be aware of. That is why the defender moves to the other side – the attacker's right. It is very difficult for

Ukenagashi, *the high level parry, done by Tomas Ohlsson of the Enighet dojo in Malmö, Sweden. Photo by the author.*

the attacker, having turned to the left for the next cut, to suddenly turn back toward the right.

In aikiken exercises, I have often seen a lack of awareness of this: The attacker sort of blindly goes on to attack in the direction the defender was at the beginning, but never returns to. Not much point in that. An attacker takes aim right before the new cut. The defender has to move accordingly.

So, one of the key intentions of the ura exercise is to make the student conscious of these dynamics, in the change of directions between attacker and defender.

At *chiburi*, shaking off the blood, the defender starts with a step back, so as not to be unbalanced when doing the chiburi movement. This is also something the student needs to be aware of: At an extended stance with the left foot forward, there is a lack of balance if pulled even slightly to the forward right (and vice versa). Every stance has its strong and weak points. With this adaption of the chiburi, that important fact is pointed out.

7 Chudan

Leaving the ukenagashi, we now study *kote*, the wrist cut, in a pair of exercises. Kote is well appreciated in kendo, certainly, but I believe that in other sword arts – also in aikiken – its efficiency is usually underestimated. The  swordsman needs the sword, and the sword depends on the hands. Still, the wrists are actually the least protected in the guards and movements of the sword arts. Terrific targets, then, and often more easy to get at than any other part of the body.

In this pair of exercises, I also put attention to the two most important levels – *chudan* and *jodan*. Since kote is a small target, it is very important to know where to find it, when the attacker holds the sword at different heights. Practicing the kote cut, you become quite aware of the difference of chudan and jodan – they feel like a mile apart.

The chudan exercise is to me pretty much a *mae*, with just another timing to it. If the attacker charges too quickly for the defender to both draw and cut before the attacker's cut is completed – then kote chudan is an alternative, allowing the defender some more time, though not a lot of it. In the sword arts, there is never a lot of time.

The first move is simply a step to the left, out of the way of the attacking sword, and a simultaneous draw. Then the kote.

The exercise could very well end there, with the idea of cutting through the attacker's wrist and be done with it. But the attacker is likely to have two arms, so there could be a one-handed attack, *katate*, following. That is why the exercise goes on. It must be understood that kote is never a final technique.

And here comes a manoeuver which might have more relevance to the aikidoka than to the swordsman, nevertheless practical to both. The defender is using the sword to control the attacker's next move, to sort of guide it. This way, the attacker has little else to do than draw to jodan for a new cut, and by this opens for *yokomen*, a side cut to the head.

The reason for yokomen is primarily in how the sword is moved previously. The most natural follow-up is yokomen. But of course, there is also a need for exercising this important cut when given a good chance.

The *chiburi* used here, a well known one indeed, I find ideal to perform after a yokomen. Actually, I think they suit each other so well, the yokomen and this chiburi, that the combination should be used for anyone wanting to learn this very difficult, rather awkward chiburi.

In this exercise, the attacker starts from *miginowaki*, a right side guard, after having done pretty much the same thing in the previous six exercises. Time for a change, no doubt. For the defender it is good to experience the slightly different timing of this attack. Furthermore, there is an interesting contrast between the great force of the attack from the side guard, and the precise technique of the kote cut, saying something about how the small conquers the big, the soft surpasses the hard, and so forth.

A later interpretation of the five guards of Musashi. What he describes in the Book of Five Rings, though, seems to be something different, and not with two swords.

8   Jodan

This exercise is inspired by Miyamoto Musashi. He describes something like it in his *Go Rin no Sho*, Book of Five Rings, among the very few techniques he actually mentions in any detail. It is a bit dangerous to practice. With Musashi at its root, that can come as no surprise. So, caution is needed.

What is most rewarding here, is the understanding it gives to timing. The defender's sword should hit the attacker's wrist just as the arm is coming down in the attacking cut. Not too early, or you miss the kote, and not too late, or the angle will not be good enough to cut through. At the optimal moment, the attacker unwillingly helps with the kote cut.

Angles are important. The defender's sword must be extended to hit with the correct section of the blade, slightly below the tip of it, *kissaki*. It also has to be done when the angle between the defender's arm and sword is such that the cut is strong. This takes some training, but the student learns so much about the sword arts in the process.

I really have a feeling that if this move cannot be properly executed by the student, then he or she is really unable to do a lot of other things with the sword, which may seem easy enough.

When it comes to the final cut, *yokomen*, I allowed myself to introduce another difficulty, which might be a bit out of touch with the shoden basic thinking otherwise applied. The easiest would probably be to allow the sword to continue after the cote cut, and spin around at the end of it. Instead it is stopped after kote, and then flipped.

There is a basic teaching aspect to this choice: If allowed to continue the cut and spin the sword around, the student will not be able to perceive how precise the kote actually was - in what angle the sword hit the wrist, with what strength, and so forth. Stopping the sword right after it, will make that obvious.

And with the following yokomen, the student needs to learn how to make a strong cut although not having a lot of distance to accelerate the sword – a bit like the one inch punch of fist fighting arts. It takes precision, focus, a good center, and a lot of practice. I can't say that I master it myself, in case you wondered – but I have great fun trying.

9   Ate

The last pair of exercises in the aikibatto shoden, focuses on *harai*, also pronounced *barai*, the warding off. This can be done in a number of ways, for example as in the *ukenagashi* of  exercises five and six, where the blade is used. Here, though, the harai is done with *tsuka*, the hilt, as the sword is not yet drawn.

This may not be a very commonly used technique in the

sword arts, for the simple reason that the sword is drawn as quickly as possible, often before the first attack. But in the typical iaido case, and in aikibatto, where the defender always starts with the sword in the scabbard, some techniques with the hilt should be practiced.

I take the opportunity to introduce another attacking technique as well: *tsuki*, the thrust. Although it is a basic technique with the sword, and a very efficient one at that, my experience is that defense against it is not practiced nearly enough in regular aikiken.

Dealing with a tsuki attack can be very tricky indeed. The timing is different from that in a cut. Many aikido students are so used to practicing defense against a cut, that they cannot even imagine a tsuki coming. They allow themselves to stand too near the attacker's sword to begin with. Too late do they perceive that what is coming is a thrust, not the draw for a cut. The tip of the sword in a *chudankamae* position must be respected, and training defense against tsuki accomplishes just that – very quickly, too. It also teaches the student to establish a proper *maai*, distance, to the attacker.

Actually, as can be detected from the above, I regard the defense training against a tsuki attack more important in these last two exercises, than the actual harai being used. Because tsuki can be quite a surprise, and usually leaves less time to act for the defender than a big cut does, the warding off is done with the defender's sword still in the scabbard.

In the first of the two exercises, the student learns that also the undrawn sword can be used as a weapon. *Ate*, the hit, is done with the tsuka. When the sword is used this way, it is important to keep the sword firmly in the scabbard, or there can be all kinds of mishaps. That, too, is good to familiarize oneself with, as an example of optimizing an alternative road of action.

The ate here is both a strike at the attacker, and a way of pushing him or her back, to give room for drawing the sword. Since these movements need to be done swiftly, and with the attacker close by, it is a good situation to apply the left hand support of the blade in *yokogiri*, the side cut, to give it some additional strength and stability. Again, this is a way of optimizing a rather unusual road of action.

The *chiburi* used here, I find particularly suitable for a chudankamae position, whether it be reached with a cut, as here, or a tsuki, as in the final exercise. I have chosen the way to do this *noto* that I was taught by Nishio sensei. I find it more controlled and safe than other solutions for it.

10   Tsuki

In the last exercise, *harai* is done on the other side of the attacker's sword, and this time the defender gets to respond with *tsuki*, the thrust.

One of the things to practice here, is the draw of the sword, which should be in smooth continuance of the harai. Because of the position of the sword after this type of draw, tsuki comes naturally. Similar to the case of *jodankote* in exercise eight, the attacker rushes into the technique, thereby unwillingly helping it. An understanding of timing is needed to make this work well.

The ninth and tenth exercise are a bit more out of the ordinary than, say, the first four, and this is intentional. Actually, I hope that the series of ten exercises works as an escalation of complexity and technical difficulty.

Of course, in the sword arts there is nothing more essential or difficult, than learning the basic cut properly. But for the students it is of some attraction, if they can feel that they move toward more intricate ways of using the sword. It also has the advantage of preparing them for the okuden series, which I plan to add, given time.

Aikibatto jo. The eighth exercise, kote jodan. *In the jo form, there is a strike to the throat instead of the wrist cut in the sword form.*

Jo

The set of ten *jo*, staff, exercises is an addition that I made a year after constructing the shoden sword exercises. They are as close to the sword exercises as possible with a jo, and should be regarded as secondary.

Aikibatto is primarily a system of sword exercises. The jo set is added to give students an introduction to how the jo is to be used. That is why I have not spent as many words on this part of aikibatto.

I doubt that I will make an okuden set of jo exercises, but it is not completely out of the question.

Okuden

Just a few words about the *okuden* series that I have yet to make. It will be ten exercises, evenly divided into two groups: *nagare* and *taninzugake*.

Nagare is floating or flowing, as in *kinagare* often used in aikido for continuous execution of techniques without pauses. The five nagare exercises will have multiple movements for both tori and uke. Not too many exchanges of blows and parries, since that is impractical and quite unrealistic, but certainly more than in the shoden series.

The set will surely begin with an exercise from *seiza*, a seated position. Most iaido traditions have several such forms, so there should be at least one in aikibatto, to get the students familiar with it. Maybe there will also be one with another way of sitting than seiza, such as *iaihiza*, as in the fourth form of *Seitei iai*. The nagare set will also include *hasso*, the shoulder guard, which is nowhere in the shoden set. Maybe also *gedankamae*, the low guard, if it does not fit better in the taninzugake exercises. There will also be some less common draws and cuts, but probably no additional form of chiburi.

Taninzugake is defense against several attackers. This is common in iaido, of course, and supposed to be in aikido as well. The five exercises of taninzugake will include defense against two, three, and four attackers, but there is not much point in having more attackers than that. Probably the first two exercises will be against two attackers, the third against three, and the last two against four.

Some uncommon draws and cuts will be used, but not too much. Taninzugake is difficult enough as it is. The most important thing is to learn to make strategically efficient *taisabaki* evasive movements. Also, the students should exercise how to move from one strike to the next, without unnecessary movements of the sword. That is: Each strike should end in a position that is a kind of *kamae*, from which next strike can be immediate.

Just as with the shoden set, I want the okuden set to be possible to train solo with shinken or iaito, as well as with partners and bokken. That will surely lead to some complications in the taninzugake exercises, but obstacles are there to be overcome.

I have one major reason for not having completed the okuden set of aikibatto exercises yet. I introduced the shoden set in the year 2000, and since then it is more or less regularly trained in our dojo. When observing the students, I found no need to add the okuden set. They had enough to work with as it was. I still feel that way. The shoden set seems to be quite enough to work with for a number of years. So, I will hurry to complete the okuden set when my students appear to be in need of it. This is approaching, though not imminent.

Spiritual aspects

The essence of budo training is refinement of the spirit. That is certainly true for its sword arts as well. Any book on the Japanese sword arts would be incomplete without some mention of the spiritual aspects.

The sword is a mighty symbol in Japanese culture, since legendary times. The sharpened and polished steel represents a pure spirit and a straight path. There is no point in training iaido, aikiken, or aikibatto, without that in mind.

This book has no room for going through all the spiritual aspects in depth, but I will try to present some of the fundamentals. They should be the core of your everyday training.

Do – the way

Before the 19th century, most martial arts in Japan had the suffix *jutsu*, meaning technique, skill, or art. The sword arts were called kenjutsu and battojutsu, the unarmed arts jujutsu, and so on. The essence of those arts was the ability to apply them to battle.

In the Meiji restoration of 1868, the emperor took over the power from the shogun, thereby ending the samurai era. When the samurai lost their elevated position in the country, so did their arts. They had become obsolete as methods of battle, and they lost their importance as skills for a ruling class, since that class no longer ruled.

But Japanese society appreciated the value of those old arts, and soon made measures to have them preserved and practiced – though not just by the samurai, but by any Japanese citizens, and not for their martial aspects, but for the good they did to the souls and bodies of those training them.

The latter called for a change of attitude to the martial arts. They were not to be trained for martial skills, but for personal refinement and development. So, one after the other was modified, and changed suffix from jutsu to *do*, way or path – also pronounced *michi*. Jujutsu became judo, and so on. The old forms were still around, but rather seclusively, whereas the new forms soon became popular sports.

This transformation is important to be aware of, when training the Japanese martial arts. Of course, they should still be relevant and functional in their martial aspects – such as self defense. But there is something else that is of far greater importance: They should refine the minds and bodies of their practitioners, and help them on their paths of personal development.

One needs a *do* by which to pursue one's self-realization, one's personal growth. Without it, one can only think about it. In the Eastern mind, thinking is not enough for a person to develop. One needs to act, as well. The mind must join with the body, for the whole human being to evolve.

In sword art training, we struggle to develop the practical skills, but in this process we also sharpen our minds and refine our spirits. That's what the training is really about.

One could say that the technical skills are *omote*, on the surface, but the spiritual development is *ura*, what happens inside. Another way of putting it is that the physical training is *shoden*, the first mediation, whereas the mental training is *okuden*, the inner mediation. But that is little more than playing with words. No matter how it is described, the students must understand that the whole point of training is the mental and spiritual development.

It will lead to better skills, as well, but that is secondary.

To remain true to the path when training, means that one should not regard winning over others as any significant progress. It is far more rewarding to think of the others as

Scene from the kabuki play Chushingura, *about the 47 ronin who sacrificed their lives in order to avenge their master. Wood print,* ukiyo-e, *by Kuniteru (Sadashige), 1855.*

fellow travelers on the path, helping each other along the way. In a *dojo,* the place where a *do* is practiced, every member of it should develop, or none of them can reach any height.

Being true to the path also consists of not settling with having one's mere technical skills improve, but to search inside for what is really expressed through them. Although it is a martial art, it should be trained with peacefulness in mind, and a beneficial spirit. Even when swinging the sword in a mighty strike, one should do it in a spirit of perfection, rather than destruction.

Attitude

There are countless ways in which one's attitude influences one's martial art. Therefore, it is always important to work on refining one's attitude, and not be blinded by focusing on the physical results. It is an inward process, not an outward one.

For the beginner, the sharpness of the sword helps the mind to sharpen, but for the advanced student it should be the other way around – the sharpness of the mind is what makes the sword sharp. The aim of the training is to create and improve the sharpness of the mind, whereas the increased sharpness of one's sword should be regarded as little more than a side-effect.

Attitude is a good concept to consider, when pursuing one's path. The general attitude should be one of relaxation and clarity, with no particular goal in sight, nor anything specific that one is desperate to protect. Just being, *ima* (the first 'i' in iaido), and perfectly free to adapt to any circumstance. You could call it empty mind.

Then, through the movements of a kata or exercise, one's attitude changes according to what is done at the moment. It is a kind of mental process, going through several stages:

In the first step of a iaido kata, or an aikibatto solo exercise, nothing happens. This step should be taken with the original attitude of empty mind, complete openness, with neither plan nor goal.

At the next step, the attacker charges, and you go for your sword. Here, the attitude immediately changes into one of complete awareness and focus. You should have a strong spirit forward, as if intending to walk right through the attacker.

The following step is where you do your *taisabaki* evasive movement, and you draw your sword. Here, you should actually have an attitude of letting the attacker's force through, of sort of helping the attacker along. This is the *aiki* choice, not blocking the attacking energy but joining with it. Even if you strike the attacker in this step, you should have the same attitude.

Next is the movement where you strike down the attacker. This should be done in an attitude of returning to the attacker what he or she released in the attack. Giving back – not as a revenge, but as a kindness, bringing things back to order. One could also say that you bring the attacker's intention to completion. The attacker intended to strike, therefore you do, so that not even the intention is lost.

The moment before the draw. From a 2002 seminar in Plzen, Czech Republic. Photo by Larry Kwolek.

You accepted the charge in the previous step, and you accept the underlying intention in this step.

It should be done without any aggression. That does not mean without power, but completely without aggression, without a destructive will.

Ichimura sensei used to talk about 'the sword that gives life', by which I believe he referred to the attitude in this step. You should not strike with the desire to stop the attacker, but with the will to bring him or her to completion.

Nishio sensei had another way of treating this step. He stopped the strike right before it would hit, as a way of showing the attacker the consequences of his or her action, but still giving the attacker a chance to reconsider and retreat. He talked about this very often, and *aikido toho*, his own iai system, was full of examples of it.

For your development in this *do*, it is extremely important not to see the strike as a way of striking down the attacker, but as a way of bringing him or her back to order. Back to square one, so to speak – as if there had not been an attack at all. You can also say that this is a way to free the attacker from any guilt or *karma* of what has passed.

Either the strike ends in one or other *kamae*, guard position, or you move your sword to one. This kamae is held for a little while, in a spirit of expanding one's awareness all around. No doubt, the spirit has been focused on the attacker up to this point. So, it is important to open up and spread one's awareness, in case other attackers might follow – but more essentially, this is a first step back to the empty mind attitude.

During this moment, you look down at the fallen attacker. Traditionally, this is to check that he or she is completely incapacitated – or dead. In modern training there is nobody there, of course, so the best way is to look down to conclude that no one has been harmed, and that things have indeed come to their conclusion. You brought things to their conclusion in the strike, so at this moment you simply ascertain that you did.

Still, you should remain alert in your extended awareness. It is like a sphere that you expand all around you. Make the sphere as big as you feel that you manage. Do not stare very intently on the floor in front of you, but gaze with an open mind. If you remain in the focused spirit you had at the previous strike, you will be ignorant of anything else happening around you, and that is a weakness.

When you have ascertained that completion is reached, and no other attackers approach, you can do *chiburi*, the movement for shaking off the blood from the sword. The original intention of the movement was just that: to shake off the attacker's blood, although the blade also had to be wiped. In modern training, though, another shaking off is intended: that of the deed, of what just passed. You need to let it pass, get it out of your mind, so that it does not disturb you onward. Symbolically, any guilt or *karma* is washed off by this movement. You open up, and become peaceful again.

It is evident in the actual movement. Your right hand makes chiburi to the right with the sword, and your left hand goes to the *saya*, scabbard, on your left. Your belly, more specifically your center, is exposed. You show yourself, instead of your sword. The high energy that you had charged yourself with for the battle, is released and flows

78   Aikibatto

out of you. You remain in the middle, and become calm. Just like you clean the blade with the chiburi movement, you clean yourself from the battle, as if it never happened. Forget it, so that you can move on. Otherwise, the only one harmed by the exercise is you.

Noto, shielding the sword, should be done with the attitude of bringing everything back to *tanden*, your center. It is a peaceful thing, bringing you to completion. At the strike you brought your attacker to completion, and by noto you do the same for yourself. Therefore, whatever noto you do, make sure that it is full of the spirit of returning to your center. So, it is good if the tsuba and the saya meet right in front of your center.

Then you put your left hand thumb on the tsuba, and let your right hand slide up to *kashira*, the end piece of the hilt. At the same time, and in the same tempo, you look up. Also, you push the sword slightly to the left, so that kashira gets in front of your center – the same position it should have when you start an exercise. Both hands cooperate in pushing the sword firmly into the scabbard.

Looking up, it is like you see the world anew. What preceded it, you have forgotten, and what's ahead of you, you are completely open to. When you lower your right hand, you should delight in this sensation of fresh openness. Continue in this spirit as you go back to your starting point.

When your left hand releases its grip on the scabbard, and slides down to your side, you should have forgotten the previous events completely. It is like you have just woken up to a new day. You are back in empty mind.

These changes of attitude through the movements of the exercise, apply not only to the sword arts, but relate also to how you should learn to live your life as a whole. So, don't worry about things before they happen, but immediately focus and move to action when they do. Bring things to completion. Bring yourself to peace afterward, and let go of what has passed as if it never did. Again and again through life, it is the same. The cycle is repeated – sometimes like thunder, sometimes like a whisper. If your sword art training makes you increasingly competent at handling such cycles, it is indeed your path.

I should mention that in *kinagare* aikido training, where there is no stopping, the steps and attitude changes above are not relevant. In short, you should remain throughout in the third attitude, that of letting the attacker's spirit pass, of helping it to pass. In *jutai* training, though, you follow approximately the same steps as described for the sword arts above.

Tanden – the center

Tanden, the center, is central in all budo. This point, about an inch below the navel, in the middle of your body, is where all movements should commence as well as end up.

It is called *kikai tanden*, the ocean of ki in the abdomen. It is also called *seika tanden*, the energy field below the navel, or *seika no itten*, the point below the navel. In budo, when you need power, this is where you get it. Balance, too. And here is where you do your power breathing, *kokyuryoku*. In the Indian *chakra* system, this is the second chakra from the bottom, *svadhisthana*.

The kanji for tanden consists of two signs, the first means red and the second means rice field. The red rice field. To the Chinese (in China it is pronounced *dantian*) and the Japanese, the rice field is a mighty symbol of vital nourishment. When it is red, that nourishment is particularly powerful. So, tanden is the center of power.

But it is more than that. It is the middle of one's own universe, where everything begins and ends, and really remains also in between. Therefore, when working on your own development, you should concentrate on your center, and when interacting with your partner, focus on his or her center.

In the Japanese sword arts, the importance of the center is quite evident. The field marshal of the guards, *chudan-kamae*, is to hold the sword in front of your center. In a *chudangiri* strike with the sword, you pull the sword up in a forward movement, extending from your center, and cut by bringing it back the same way, to your center. It is the same with *tsuki*, the thrust, where you extend the sword forward from your center, and then bring it back the same way. So, basic sword exercises are excellent for developing your sense of center, and making it grow.

Every movement, at least if it is to be of any significance and power, commences in the center. That is why you should focus on the attacker's center – not the sword, or the arms, or the eyes. If you connect to uke's center, you will sense the charges right before uke starts moving, at the moment when uke decides to go. That decision may be done by the brain, but the body movement needs to begin in the center.

When intention shall become action, it needs to go through the center. You can notice it, if you focus on it. The only way for the center not to reveal the intention, is if it is not involved. In that case the action is weak and uncommitted.

This is also one of the reasons why the attacker is really at such a disadvantage. Someone who wants to initiate by attacking, is not able to tune in to the opponent's center, because of the decision forming in one's own center. When attacking, one is trapped within one's own center, or one would not be able to attack fiercely. The defender, on the other hand, is open to sense the opponent's center, and can react by mirroring its initiatives. A response is perceptive, but a charge is not.

If you allow yourself to leave your center, for example by adding mental ambition to your technique, you will lose balance and force. It will be like stumbling, and your arms will flap uncontrollably in the struggle to regain body balance. So, remain always in your center, and let your techniques be nothing but expressions of it – eruptions from the center that you never lure yourself to follow.

It is only by solidly remaining in your center that you can have the attitude of empty mind, or the extended awareness, mentioned above. Osensei talked about being in one's own universe. Having your own universe is being in the middle of it, and that is being in your center. Koichi Tohei, the founder of *Ki no Kenkyukai*, has also said much about the center, but this is not an aikido invention. All the Japanese and Chinese martial arts are quite aware of it, and have been for ages.

The center becomes more and more, as you continue to advance on your budo path. It is your inner temple, it is the source out of which your techniques get their forms, and it is the birth place of *takemusu*, improvised budo. If you do not concentrate on your center in your budo training, it is not budo you are training. Remaining in your center also means always to focus on it, always to allow it to be the hub of your wheel of progress. Then you cannot get lost on the way.

You will not go wrong if you see all that you do in your training as expressions of your center.

Ki – life energy

Ki, the life force, is the middle character in the kanji for aikido. Still, many teachers and students of aikido hesitate to include it in their training – probably because it is a vague and esoteric thing. But without it, aikido or any other budo lacks an essential part. However uncertain you are of this ki thing, you need to incorporate it in your training, in whatever way you relate to it.

The word relates to air and breathing, just like the word spirit does. In the most basic way to regard it, you can say that ki is a way of breathing. Well, you die if you don't breathe. And working on your breathing does in itself work wonders with your budo development. Also, it stimulates your ki flow.

The kanji for ki combines the sign for vapor or mist, with that of rice. Just as with the kanji for *tanden*, the center, rice is used symbolically to indicate nutrition, a vital ingredient. So, ki could be interpreted as signifying the essence in air that keeps you alive. That would be oxygen.

Maybe ki is simply an ancient way of trying to describe

Osensei Morihei Ueshiba (1883-1969), the founder of aikido, throwing without touching. It can be explained as an application of kokyuryoku, *power breath. Photo, courtesy of Yasuo Kobayashi.*

oxygen, the component in air that we need for our survival. Or maybe there actually is a cosmic energy or ether of sorts, which is the real force that makes us live and move.

Whether you believe in the existence of ki or not, you can use the concept and its techniques in your budo training, and it will make you progress.

I like to call it the ether of intention. To live is to do things, and to do things you must have intention. Its fuel is ki. When you have an intention, it needs to get a direction, and your ki will flow that way. By stimulating your ki flow, you can make your intention stronger and sharper, and improve your capacity. By being sensitive to the attacker's ki flow, you can counter with greater ease, and redirect the attacker's intention.

Breathing

A good introduction to ki use and ki awareness, is working with your breathing. You need to learn to breathe with you center – that is belly breathing, also called diaphragm breathing, making your inhalations and exhalations with your abdomen. This deep power breathing, *kokyuryoku*, should become a habit, so that you do it without thinking about it. That takes some time to reach.

Think of your movements as breathing, where especially your exhalations have directions. Most techniques in budo are done with exhalation, where you are the strongest.

Actually, you can focus on exhalations and pretty much forget about inhalations. The body will manage the latter by itself. If you concentrate on extended exhalations, the inhalations done by body reflexes will be short and yet sufficient, indeed.

This also decreases the risk of getting out of breath, even when you exercise with great intensity. Often, students get out of breath because they have a reflex of shortening their exhalations in their hurry to inhale anew, when they get exhausted. But that gives little oxygen. You need to breathe out substantially, to get room in your lungs for fresh air. So, when you get out of breath, concentrate on breathing out – very much – and each inhalation will give you more than enough oxygen to keep going.

A good budo way of breathing is to make the exhalations long, and the inhalations quick. I mean really long, and really quick.

Ichimura sensei said that a iaido form, from the draw of the sword to the sheathing of it, should be done in one breath – one cycle of breathing in and out. That is an interesting way of training kata, but to learn how to use power breathing it might be more beneficial for a beginner to explore and utilize the differences between inhalation and exhalation in the movements.

When you inhale, you are significantly weaker than when exhaling, so it is important to learn when to do what, through a kata or exercise. Also, some body movements are more natural to do with an exhalation, and others with an inhalation. The more your breathing agrees with your body movements, the more effective they will be.

For example, when you lift the sword to *jodan* level before cutting with it, an inhalation is natural. And when you do the cut, the exhalation is just as natural. Actually, any lifting of the arms invites an inhalation, and lowering them does the opposite.

In a normal iaido form, you start by grabbing the sword, together with a quick inhalation. You draw it and strike, *nukitsuke*, with an exhalation. As mentioned above, you lift the sword with an inhalation, and strike with an exhalation. When you turn the sword to do *chiburi*, you inhale, and when you do the chiburi you exhale. When you swing the sword to the scabbard, you inhale, and when you sheathe it in *noto* you exhale.

The rhythm in this way of doing iaido is one of long exhalations and quick inhalations. This should be emphasized. Extend your exhalations, and shorten your inhalations.

When you do a cut or a thrust, do not stop your exhalation just because the sword stops. Keep it going, until it is time for your next movement. This is to extend your breath.

Futaridori, *two attackers. This is one of Nishio sensei's* Aikido Toho *forms. From a 2005 Berlin seminar. Photo by Frank Weingärtner.*

Also, and very importantly, start your exhalation before you start moving the sword in the strike. Otherwise the sword movement will be unstable and imprecise.

If you move very quickly from one strike to the next, you make two exhalations in a row, without inhaling in between. Don't worry, you have enough air in your lungs for that. You can do a number of exhalations before you need to inhale. It is not more complicated than for a singer to sing several tones before inhaling.

Extend ki

The inhalations correspond to receiving ki, and the exhalations to extending it. In your training, try to focus increasingly on the ki flow, instead of on the air you breathe. They are related, but they are not the same. Ki is the spirit of breath, the idea of breath, the universal principle that is expressed in breathing but also in many other ways. It is the essence of breath, of the cyclic process that keeps us alive.

You really do not need to focus on receiving ki. When you extend ki, you will by this be filled with new ki. That is one of the reasons for not focusing on inhalations, but on exhalations. Only if you stop to extend ki will you stop receiving it.

Since ki and air are not the same, they work differently behind the similarities. Therefore, it is not necessary to exhale when you extend ki, and inhale when you receive it. You can breath in at the same time as your ki extends, and vice versa. But that can be quite confusing to the beginner, who is better served by letting his or her breath and ki do the same.

When you extend ki, and thereby receive new ki, this is the essence of *misogi*, purification. Cleansing. Ki should constantly flow through you – in and out, so that the difference between the two loses distinction. When you involve yourself in action, you gather and aim your ki, but otherwise it should just flow through you constantly, without target. That is also how you should be in aikido's *kinagare*, on an advanced level.

When you accept the cleansing of the ki flow, your attitude will relax and your spirit will be increasingly refined. It can be compared to the empty mind mentioned above. Universal ki flows through you, and you are at peace within this.

Sword art fundamentals

The Japanese sword is an extremely sophisticated weapon, produced in very elaborate ways toward a rarely seen level of perfection. The same is true about the arts of handling the sword. Nothing is ignored, nothing omitted or arbitrary. The Japanese sword arts are trained with a similar sharpness in mind, as that of the blade.

It takes long to make such a sword, and it takes a life-time to handle it perfectly. I have not yet spent the time to describe all the aspects of the sword arts, nor would I have room for it in this one book. But a few practical fundamentals need to be mentioned. They deal with such basic things as how to grip the sword, and how to swing it.

Hopefully, you will find out all the rest by persistent practice, and the instructions from your teacher.

Posture

Practitioners of both kendo and iaido usually have a strikingly straight posture, and they keep it whatever they do in their training. Posture is indeed fundamental in the Japanese sword arts, a posture as uncompromising as the shape of the steel blade.

The correct posture in the sword arts is similar to that of zen meditation. The back should be straight, the shoulders relaxed and extended to the sides, the chin lowered.

The lowered chin is not of particular value in itself, but a result of the head held in such an angle that the fontanel is the highest point of it. That way, your central pillar is straight all the way from the bottom of your torso to the top of your head. You should feel like a pillar, and energy should flow through it – both upward and downward, from *tanden*,

Kendo seminar in Malmö, Sweden. Photo by the author.

your center. The downward flow increases your balance and stability, the upward flow gives you pride and authority.

The best way to adjust your body posture, is to lie down on the floor. You lie on your back, arms by your sides, feet at about shoulder distance. There you relax, and allow gravity to pull you to the floor. After a minute or so, you stand up and try to keep exactly the posture you had lying down. This very simple exercise can be repeated as you please, and you will be surprised by how much it improves your posture.

When you train in the dojo, whether it is sword exercises or aikido, you should check your posture now and then. Even if it was perfect at the outset, it could happen that you start crouching after a while, quite unawares. This easily happens in suburi training.

You should be able to do all the techniques and exercises without losing posture – especially in the sword arts. Make the sword an expression of yourself, not a tool that sort of takes over and makes you dependent of it. If you think of the sword as an extension of your arm, you will have an attitude that helps to preserve your straight posture.

The power of your movements should come from

tanden, your center in the abdomen. But do not let your belly protrude, and your hips tilt forward, in an effort to accentuate your center. That makes the posture flawed. It is also quite demanding on your lower back, at length. Keep your straight posture, and your hips in a vertical position, although you do your movements with power from your center.

The best way to keep your posture when you act, is to always extend energy through your central pillar, at the same time as you make your technique. In a basic cut with the sword, extend energy forward from the center for the cut, but also extend energy upward and downward through your pillar. So, when you do something, your energy simultaneously goes in three directions: forward, upward, and downward. That will keep your posture straight, and assure that you have the stability needed for your technique.

Grip

How you grip the sword is essential in the Japanese sword arts. It is almost an art in itself. Normally, you grip it with both hands, where the left one is closer to *kashira*, the end piece of the hilt, and the right is closer to *tsuba*, the sword guard.

This is not so much a right-handed thing, as it is related to the basic stance with the right foot forward. The symmetry between hands and feet adds capacity and power. Traditionally, it may also be a way of protecting the heart, by turning the right side forward.

Some choose to grab the actual kashira with their left hand, to increase versatility. In heavy duty suburi cutting, though, kashira tends to gnaw on the palm of your hand. Therefore, I recommend a grip where the hand is not in contact with kashira, except for certain maneuvers where you need to cup your left hand around kashira.

The same can be said about the right hand and tsuba. If you avoid pressing the index finger on the tsuba, you can more comfortably do a lot of training.

So, the hands should be placed completely on the tsuka, not sticking out over kashira, and not pressing on tsuba. But they should not be placed tightly together. There should be some distance between the hands. This distance  depends on the length of tsuka, of course, but experiment a little with what choice you have. If the hands are rather close, without actually touching each other, you may find that you gain some power and control for the regular cutting moves. On the other hand, that may make it trickier to move the sword in parries and such. Try to find a distance that works the best throughout.

Now, most important with the grip – and most complicated for beginners to learn – are the angles of the hands. You should not grip straight on, like you would an axe. Instead you twist your hands, so that your wrists turn slightly inward and to yourself. It is kind of a spiral movement with the hands, as the grip tightens. You apply your hands to the sides of tsuka, but turn them upward-inward as you tighten the grip.

This angle of the wrists puts tsuka exactly in front of your arms, so that you have the most force and stability possible. Otherwise, with the wrong angle of your wrists, it would only be the thumbs pressing the sword forward and down in your cut. With the correct grip, your sword is held to the centers of your palms, and your arms are directly in line with the cutting movement.

Students usually need to train long, to apply this grip correctly. The best way of making this natural for you, is to think of the grip as the fingers feeding the tsuka into the palms. As they squeeze the tsuka, it is pressed tighter to your palms.

The grip should not be rigid, but quite tight. Not a lot of air between the hands and tsuka. The hands should stick tightly to tsuka, like a wet rag wrapped around it.

It is difficult to explain accurately. Try it, and try to improve it. Remember to correct it frequently during training, if your grip changes along the way – and that is likely.

Finally, the fingers differ in how much strength they apply to the grip. The two little fingers are the most important of the ten – as in many other budo techniques. Actually, if you concentrate on making them grip properly and distinctly, you can forget about the other fingers. That way, you will have the correct distribution of power between the fingers.

Nishio sensei used to say that the little finger should have 50% of the total power of the grip, the ring finger 30%, and the middle finger 20%. The index finger does not grip the sword at all. This distribution is what comes when you focus only on the little finger. So, pay attention to your little fingers, and the rest will work out by itself.

Do not allow any fingers of the grip to extend and point elsewhere. They should stick to the tsuka, sort of like glued there, so that all the energy of your grip goes through the sword. Your grip should be homogenous, all of your power extending through the sword, and all your ten fingers connected to that one purpose.

The strength of the grip varies, according to what you do with it. When you strike, the grip should be strong, and increase through the strike. It is the same when you parry. At movements in between, and in *kamae* positions, the grip should be distinct, but not too strong.

At any time, at least one hand should have a fixed grip on the sword. When both hands hold it, the left hand grip is always the most important one, and should be the strongest.

At the actual cut, your grip should feel like your hands have melted into the sword, so that your arms, your hands, and your sword, are all one.

Cut

The cut is a combination of chopping and slicing: The beginning of it is a chop, sort of what you do with an axe, but then it continues with a slicing movement, all through to the end of it. At the chop, the sword is the most extended forward, and in the following slicing it is pulled closer to you, ending with the hilt in front of your center.

In samurai times, practically the whole blade was used in a cut. The slicing was done all the way from close to *tsuba*, the sword guard, and on to *kissaki*, the sword tip. So, those warriors tried to get up close to their opponents, when striking.

The sword cut is usually described as circular, but it is more accurate to call it elliptical. You extend it in the first part of the cut, and bring it back in the second. That movement forms part of an ellipse, where one of its focal points is your center, and the other is your aim – for example the opponent's head in a *men* strike.

There is a variation of speed, which can be compared to that of celestial bodies in elliptical orbits around the sun. They accelerate when they travel toward the sun, which is one of the focal points of the orbit, and decelerate when they move away from it. A sword cut should be the same: the sword accelerates all the way to the strike, the chopping part of the cut, and then decelerates in the continuing slicing movement back to you.

You should not intentionally slow the sword down in the second part of the cut, but this will naturally happen. If you just focus on having a maximum acceleration at the moment of the strike, the rest will take care of itself.

Do not make your aim such that your speed would be the highest at the end of the cut, when the sword is about to stop. It needs to be the fastest at the striking point, when it reaches the opponent. After the moment of penetration it cuts with the sharpness of the edge, more than the speed of it.

A good way of learning this rhythm of cutting, is to think of a men cut only, but allowing the sword to continue all the way to *gedan*, the low level. But think men, and not gedan, do not add energy to your cut after the men level. You will soon find the rhythm of it, and you also learn a very relaxed way of cutting.

Of course, if you actually do the men cut, you should stop at that level, and accelerate all the way to it. In men, you only do the chopping part of the cut. It is the same with *kote*, striking the wrist.

The samurai sword has a tremendous sharpness, comparable to that of a modern razorblade. This is its superior power. So, basic sword technique is simply to utilize this sharpness optimally. This means that you need to have a stable cutting movement, where the edge of the sword is exactly in line with your cutting move. Think carefully about that, when you train the sword arts. Whatever cut you do – check that you move the sword exactly in line with its edge.

This is ascertained by the grip, as well. When you have learned a correct grip of the sword, according to what is discussed above, you will find it easy to move it with accuracy.

Another way of assuring the sharpness of the cut, is by breathing: You should exhale when you cut, to have the most power in that movement, but for the stability of the cut you need to begin your exhalation before you start cutting. This is also discussed in the chapter about *ki*, the life energy.

If you start to breathe out at the same time you begin the cut, there is a risk that it will be wobbling and imprecise. With the start of an exhalation, there is too much body movement going on for you to keep precision and stability in your cut. But if you start the exhalation before the cut, it is easy to do it correctly. Practice this a lot, because it is more difficult than it might seem. Breathing is a habit that is hard to reprogram.

Your center, *tanden*, is not only one of the focal points of the elliptic cutting move. It is also the base of every move you do. This is particularly obvious in the cut: You draw the sword by extending it from your center, and you cut by pulling it back to your center – with outstretched arms. You will improve the power and control of the cut, if you think of it as almost nothing but an expression of your center. When you draw the sword, it is the center pushing it out, and when you cut, the center is pulling the sword back.

In basic suburi training, it is good to make *chudangiri*, the cut to middle level, because it lands in *chudankamae*, the guard with the sword in front of your center. That way, the center remains in focus all through the exercise.

When you let your conscious mind retreat, and allow your center to take control of your sword moves, your sword art will rush toward perfection. Well, it will still take decades, but you will be on the right track.

Aikibatto exercises

Shoden 初伝

SHIHO four directions 四方

1   MAE front 前

2   USHIRO back 後

3   HIDARI left 左

4   MIGI right 右

UKENAGASHI parry 受流

5   OMOTE straight 表

6   URA reverse 裏

KOTE wrist 小手

7   CHUDAN middle 中段

8   JODAN high 上段

HARAI ward off 払

9   ATE strike 当

10   TSUKI thrust 突

Tori: Stefan Stenudd. Uke: Tomas Ohlsson.

1 Shiho MAE

前

Starting position: Tori at left, uke at right.

1 Tori starts with bokken in belt, facing uke, feet together. Uke starts in chudankamae, sword drawn and held at middle guard, facing tori.

2 Uke steps forward with left foot, lifts sword to jodankamae, over the head.

3 Tori steps forward with left foot, nukitsuke, drawing the sword.

4 Tori steps forward to the right with the right foot, cuts one handed do, horizontal cut on waist level, while uke's arms are still over the head. Uke steps forward with right foot.

5 Uke does chudangiri, vertical cut to middle level, in the direction of tori's original position.

6 Tori lifts sword to jodankamae, over the head, and turns toward uke. Men, straight cut to the head.

7 Uke yields sword to miginowaki, right side guard. Retreats three steps.

8 Tori lowers sword to chudankamae, middle guard.

9 Tori does chiburi chudan, "shake off blood" to the right on middle level.

10 Tori does noto, sword back into scabbard. Steps back to the starting position.

Details

Shiho, four directions, is a common concept in iaido, found for example in the first four forms of *Omori ryu*. It is, of course, a way of preparing for attacks from any direction. In a more elaborate training, it can be done by *happo*, eight directions, the first four being the same as here and the next four in diagonal directions to these. In a shoden basic system, though, there is no need for more than four directions – front, back, left, right.

Seiza, the sitting position, is usually the starting point for the first few forms of a iaido kata system, but in aikibatto shoden, all exercises are performed standing up. This makes better sense in relation to most aikiken, and also to the way in which swords were used in old Japan. The samurai never wore the katana in the belt when seated.

I would not call a swordplay system with walking on one's knees an ideal start for learning the basics of sword moves, especially not for the non-Japanese, unacquainted with *suwariwaza*, the knee walking.

Mae, front, is the first of the four Shiho. Uke comes straight at tori. In most iaido schools, some kind of mae is the very first form, because of its basic character. Here in aikibatto it does not deviate much from the iaido standard, except for the *taisabaki* move to the right, taking place at the fourth movement, and the consequences of this.

Normally in iaido, *nuki-tsuke*, the draw, finishes with the sword tip in front of the left eye of uke, who has not yet drawn the sword. But here, where uke's sword is already raised, the draw is immediately followed by a cut to uke's waist in movement four, right before uke's sword comes down in chudangiri, a cut to middle level.

In the taisabaki step to the

right, of the fourth movement, it is important to let the left foot follow a bit, so that none of tori's body is in the way of uke's sword when it comes down in the fifth move. Not even the heel of the left foot.

The horizontal cut in movement four is not as easy as it may seem to the beginner, since it needs to be done so that the edge of the sword is exactly in line with the movement, that is completely horizontal. It should strike at the soft waist – between the hip bone and the lowest rib. Here, some contact is both allowed and of benefit, for checking out how the cut is performed. Make sure, beforehand, that the bokken used has no flaws on its surface that might harm uke.

Uke cuts *chudan*, to middle level, in movement five, but actually a cut to *jodan*, high level, or *gedan*, low level, would work as well – making no difference whatsoever to tori. Not even *yokomen* or *kesagiri* would cause any complications. That goes for most of the ten shoden exercises – uke's attack can usually vary without tori having to change any movement. This is of quite some importance, since it is almost impossible for tori to know what cut will come.

So, in training it can be beneficiary to the awareness of tori, if uke actually changes between cuts – sometimes chudan, sometimes jodan or gedan – but not until tori has developed some confidence in the moves.

When uke cuts in movement five, already being cut in the waist at movement four, this would for obvious reasons result in uke tipping forward somewhat, not able to maintain a straight posture. This happens although no actual cutting is done by tori when using a bokken. The move cuts uke's posture. It cuts the flow of ki through uke's central pillar, necessary to keep a straight back and neck when moving quickly or forcefully.

The fact that uke will end up bending forward is the reason for the cut in movement six being straight, not diagonal as in kesagiri. It still lands on the side of uke's neck, just as it would by kesagiri, and not on the top of uke's head. Otherwise a kesagiri would no doubt be more efficient.

Raising the sword to jodan and turning toward uke in movement six, is done simultaneously. The body turns at the same time as the sword is pulled to the jodan guard of where the body will be at the end of this step. At the very same instant when the body has reached its position, so shall the sword have done.

The cut of movement six should really be to chudan level, but in partner practice it stops right above the head if uke stands straight, or above the neck if uke is bending forward. Here, no contact is safe, so tori should stop the sword at a proper distance from uke's body.

The yielding of the sword to the right side, done by uke in movement seven, is not to a proper guard. That would make it unwise for tori to do *noto*, sheathing the sword. Instead, uke's sword drops downward, while moving toward the right side, so that the sword tip ends up near the floor. Uke's attitude should be relaxed, calmly surrendering. Having retreated three steps, uke waits for tori to do movements eight to ten.

Usually in aikiken, this ritualized ending is not performed, and it can become tiring at length. But being able to do it is very good for developing sharpened awareness and concentration throughout the exercise.

Tori's lowering of the sword in movement eight is done in a spirit of continued domination of the situation. The *chudankamae* guard at the end of it should be alert, with an ability to immediately charge anew.

At the *chiburi* in movement nine, the alertness is thrown away with the imaginary blood on the blade. It empties the mind of the previous duel, with an attitude of opening oneself up. This is the most basic of the many chiburi  to be found in iaido. The sword is thrust to the right, with the edge of the blade in that exact direction, to get the blood off. The blade is not horizontal, but tipping a little downward, or the blood might pour onto tori's hands.

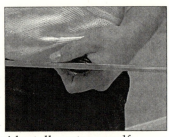

Noto, sheathing the sword, is done in just as numerous ways as chiburi, and always related to the sort of chiburi chosen. With a sharp blade, one should take care, because it is usually in noto that one accidentally cuts oneself.

When done with a bokken, the left hand forms into an opening – just as it would on the top of *saya*, the scabbard. It is not held by the side of tori's body, but immediately in front of tori's center, *tanden*. The sword slides with the back of the blade on this opening – more precisely in a track formed by the thumb and index finger. This movement is not to the side, but rather as much forward as possible, extending *tsuka*, the hilt, to the front instead of sideways. The left hand is close to the body, moving to the left. When the tip of the bokken enters the opening formed by the left hand, that hand pulls the belt a bit, for the bokken to be stuck inside of it.

When a hakama is worn, its top strap can equally well be used instead, so that the bokken will rest on the belt instead of inside it. There are several ways of doing the noto with a bokken, but this I find to be a good compromise between what's practical with the bokken and what still serves as a preparatory exercise for the proper noto with the real sword.

When noto is completed, tori moves the left foot forward to the side of the right foot, at the same time sliding with the right hand to the end of the hilt. Then the hand falls down to the side of the body in a relaxed way. At this point, tori should have let go of all that went before, as if it never happened. A completely relaxed state of mind. Then tori walks backward to the initial position.

Iai considerations

For *iai* style solo training of the tori movements in this exercise, the modifications of the above would be only three: The *do* cut in movement four should be fully extended, cutting through, and the *men* of movement six should cut through to chudan level, that is to the chudankamae position. Finally, in the *noto*, returning the blade to its scabbard, the left hand stays on the scabbard until the blade is completely sheathed. Then the thumb on the tsuba is used to press it in the last bit, at the same time as the right hand reaches *kashira*, the end piece of the hilt.

Uke's movements in this or any other aikibatto exercise are not very meaningful to practice in a iai solo style.

2 Shiho USHIRO

後

Starting position: Tori at left, uke at right.

1 Tori starts with bokken in belt, back turned to uke. Uke starts in chudankamae, sword drawn and held at middle guard, behind tori.

2 Uke steps forward with left foot, lifts sword to jodan-kamae, over the head.

3 Tori steps forward with left foot, then right foot forward to the right. Uke steps forward with right foot.

4 Uke makes chudangiri, cut to middle level, in the direction of tori's original position.

5 Tori turns around on the spot, then the nukitsuke draw. Uke takes a short step back, draws sword to jodankamae. Steps forward with the right foot.

6 Tori steps forward to the right with the right foot, cuts one handed do, side cut on waist level.

7 Uke makes chudangiri, cut to middle level, in the direction of tori's former position.

8 Tori lifts sword to jodan-kamae, over the head, and turns toward uke. Men, straight cut to the head.

9 Uke yields sword to miginowaki, right side guard. Retreats three steps.

10 Tori lowers sword to chudankamae, middle guard.

11 Chiburi chudan, "shake off blood" to the right on middle level.

12 Noto, sword back into scabbard. Step back to the starting position.

Details

Aspects and considerations already treated in the previous exercise of aikibatto, are omitted here. *Shiho,* four directions, is commented in the text on mae.

Ushiro, back, is the second of the four shiho, with uke attacking tori from behind. As well as with mae, most iaido schools have some application for this situation, and again the main deviation in aikibatto from those, is the *taisabaki* movement and its consequences. From the moment of the draw in movement five, this exercise continues the same way as mae.

At the start of the exercise, when uke stands behind tori, there should be enough of a distance between them for tori to stand a chance of finding the best timing for the steps of movement three.

In basic training of this exercise, tori should make sure to have uke in view at the start, although only in the corner of the eye. An advanced form of training this, would be for tori to look straight ahead, not seeing uke at all, and still try to move away at the right moment. It takes some awareness to accomplish, no doubt. Probably also a thick skull.

When stepping out of range in movement three, it is important to let the left foot follow a bit, so that none of that leg is in the way of uke's sword. Of course, the same goes for movement six.

Immediately after missing with the cut in movement four, uke takes about half a step back and lifts the sword to *jodankamae,* for a new cut. This should be done as if almost automatic.

Uke's second cut, in movement seven, should be directed at the place where tori was at movement five – neither at the spot which was tori's original position, nor the position tori heads for in movement six. The former of these two mistaken directions is very common, and not only among beginners.

Iai considerations

For *iai* style solo training of the tori movements in this exercise, the modifications of the above would be: Full extension of the *do* cut in movement six, and all the way to *chudan* level with the cut in movement eight. The *chiburi* and *noto* are done exactly the same way as in mae.

Uke's movements are not very meaningful to practice in a iai solo style.

3 Shiho HIDARI

左

Starting position: Tori at left, uke at right.

1 Tori starts with bokken in belt, uke on forward left. Uke starts in chudankamae, sword drawn and held at middle guard, tori on forward right.

2 Tori steps forward with right foot, into front of uke.

3 Tori turns toward uke, left foot forward, nukitsuke draw. Uke steps forward with left foot, lifts sword to jodan-kamae, over the head.

4 Tori steps forward to the right with the right foot, cuts one-handed do, side cut on waist level, sword continuing around to jodankamae. Uke steps forward with right foot.

5 Uke makes chudangiri, cut to middle level, in the direction of tori's previous position. Tori turns body to uke, left foot to right foot.

6 Immediately after uke's sword comes down, tori takes half a step back with left foot, and cuts men, straight to the head.

7 Uke yields sword to miginowaki, right side guard. Retreats three steps.

8 Tori slides left foot further back, lowers sword to gedan, the sword tip just above the floor.

9 Reverse right hand grip on the sword, flip the sword around, chiburi gedan, "shake off blood" downward.

10 Noto, sword back into scabbard. Step back to the starting position.

Details

Aspects and considerations already treated in previous exercises of aikibatto are omitted here. *Shiho*, four directions, is commented in the text on mae.

Hidari, left side, is the third of the four shiho, with uke attacking tori from the left. The position of uke could be one behind the corner of a building, in which case a movement to uke's right is out of the question. Compared to the former exercises, mae and ushiro, this one uses a more flowing sword move, as well as another *chiburi* and *noto*.

In the starting position, tori and uke are placed in sort of an L-formation, where tori has the shorter and uke the longer distance to their meeting point. It is at a right foot step that tori reaches this meeting point, in front of uke. This is the moment when they get visible to each other. At this moment uke advances. Immediately, tori turns.

When tori moves toward uke, this is done by a typical budo step, where the left foot first meets the right foot, and from there to the left, toward uke. This way, tori has better balance in the step, and many more options for how to move.

Aikibatto

Putting the feet together, almost always when there is time for it, is a good way of remaining in balance, and having the most numerous options for what to do next. For example, when uke is very near, it may be practical for tori to step back with one foot when doing a cut, but when uke is more distant, tori needs to take a step forward to reach with a cut – as in this exercise. This choice can be made instantly from the feet-together position.

In movement three, uke has raised the sword at least partly toward *jodankamae*, when tori starts the draw. Otherwise they would be in each other's way. This is also the case in the nukitsuke move of mae and ushiro, but in this exercise the timing may prove to be the most tricky one for tori.

The *do* cut in movement five is done when uke approaches, so that uke is unwillingly helping in the force and speed of the cut. Tori cuts through – with some bokken contact to uke's body, carefully applied – and continues in a wide horizontal move with the  sword, not halting the cut after it has gone past uke's body. Instead the sword moves on, and tori flips the wrist so that the edge of the sword gets to the left. The circular movement continues up to jodankamae, reaching that position at the same time as tori's body turns toward uke, bringing both feet together, in movement five.

Notice that this is different from the two previous exercises, where tori stops the sword momentarily after the *do* cut. Different lessons are to be learned: In mae and ushiro, the focus is on the horizontal cut, which is a difficult one, so it needs to be observed in order to be improved. In this exercise and the next, the focus is on swiftly reaching jodankamae, for a quick vertical cut.

The *men* cut that follows is done immediately after jodankamae is reached, preferably in a flowing way that makes the kamae position just something passed through without stop. It is still important to move the sword through the jodankamae position, or the men cut would be uncontrolled and weak. In that passing moment of the kamae, the sword is positioned by a firm grip with both hands, so that the edge gets in exact line with the following cut.

The most difficult thing with flowing sword moves between one technique and the next, is to direct the edge correctly also for the second technique. For this to be the case, one needs to make any kamae – however quickly passing – a moment to establish anew a proper sword grip and aim, which will more or less automatically adjust the direction of the edge of the sword. Actually, any position with the sword should be a sort of kamae, where the blade can immediately perform a correct cut. Usually, that means the edge should at every position in between techniques somehow point toward uke.

Uke's cut is *chudan*, to middle level, in movement five. But tori's cut is supposed to be *gedan*, to low level – although needed to stop at head level in partner practice. I have mainly two reasons for the deep gedan cut instead of chudan: Firstly, it is more relaxing and less of a tension on the back, not having to stop the sword at middle level. Secondly, it promotes a relaxed, natural, and thereby both powerful and accurate cut. Unfortunately, in partner practice the cut still has to be stopped short.

Uke needs not cut chudan in all the exercises so specifying – as mentioned also about mae. The attack can be men, gedan, even *tsuki*, the thrust, and it does not change tori's moves more than marginally.

The gedan cut is so deep that the sword stops when the point of it is only a few inches over the floor. The way to do it is not to aim toward the floor, but to extend the cut forward. Since the arms are stuck to the shoulders, this move will still lead the sword downward, all

Aikibatto

by itself. You only need to concentrate on the direction forward. This is true with any sword cut, but particularly clear with the gedan.

After movement five, uke moves the same way as in mae and ushiro, but for tori there is one more change – that of *chiburi* and the following *noto*.

Although with a partner tori must stop the cut of movement six at head level, this quick technique is meant to go all the way down to gedan level. This completion of the cut is done after uke has backed off. At the same time, in movement eight, tori slides the left foot further back to a lower, more extended stance. When making a very strong cut, this backward movement helps tremendously.

Chiburi with the sword in this low position, the point of it only an inch or so from the floor, is very reasonable to do in the following way. I learned this interesting chiburi from Nishio sensei, and I find it particularly logical when the sword is in a gedan position. I call it *chiburi gedan*, to indicate that its major activity takes place at that level.

When the sword points to the floor, release your right hand and turn it, grabbing the tsuka anew, this time with the thumb away from *tsuba*, the sword guard. Now, flip the sword around its axis, so that the edge points up, while the sword tip remains near the floor. Then, release left hand and use it to hit your right wrist from below, so that the sword is suddenly pushed up a bit. This is the actual chiburi, shaking off the blood.

Continuing with the *noto*, keep the left hand, palm down, on the spot, while the right hand pulls the sword so that the blade comes up in a horizontal position, edge out, and slides on the back of the left hand, out to the right, until the sword tip is near the opening of the scabbard. Hold the sword in the air, while the left hand grabs around the opening of the scabbard (or pulls the belt when practicing

 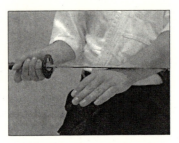

with bokken), and then let the sword slide into it. Note that when the blade is entered into the scabbard, the right hand grip on the hilt is reversed from that in chiburi chudan of the two previous exercises.

Iai considerations

For *iai* style solo training of the tori movements in this exercise, the modifications of the above would be: full extension and speed in the *do* cut of movement four, immediately continuing to *jodankamae*, and the full *gedan* cut – no stop at head height – in movements four to six.

Uke's movements in this exercise are not very meaningful to practice in a iai solo style.

4 Shiho MIGI

右

Starting position: Tori at right,
uke at left.

1 Tori starts with bokken in
belt, uke on forward right.
Uke starts in chudankamae,
sword drawn and held at
middle guard, tori on forward
left.

3 Tori turns right foot and
body toward uke, steps
forward with left foot,
nukitsuke draw. Uke steps
forward with left foot, lifts
sword to jodankamae, over
the head.

2 Tori steps forward with
right foot, into front of uke.

4 Tori slides further forward
and to the left with the left
foot, cuts one-handed do, side
cut on waist level, body
twisting sideways and sword
continuing to a horizontal
position near the body. Uke
steps forward with right foot,
makes chudangiri, cut to
middle level, in the direction
of tori's previous position.

6 Immediately after jodan-kamae, tori takes half a step back with the right foot, and strikes men, straight cut to the head.

9 Reverse right hand grip on the sword, flip the sword around, chiburi gedan, "shake off blood" downward.

5 Tori swings the sword around in a vertical circle up to jodankamae. Turns body to uke, right foot to left foot.

7 Uke yields sword to miginowaki, right side guard. Retreats three steps.

8 Tori slides right foot back, lowers sword to gedan. Left foot takes a full step back.

10 Noto, sword back into scabbard. Step back to the starting position.

Details

Aspects and considerations already treated in previous exercises of aikibatto are omitted here. *Shiho*, four directions, is commented in the text on mae.

Migi, right side, is the last of the four shiho, with uke coming at tori from the right. The position of uke could be one behind the corner of a building, in which case a movement to uke's left is awkward – therefore not used here. Just like hidari, this exercise uses a more flowing sword move, as well as another chiburi and noto, than mae and ushiro.

The starting position is like that of hidari, except for uke standing on the right instead of left side. When tori turns, in movement three, this begins by turning the right foot toward uke, which helps considerably in both turning the body and taking the following step with the left foot.

The sliding with left foot in movement four, is part of the *taisabaki* move away from the aim of uke. It should not be straight forward, but a little to the side. Not directly sideways, though, which would lead to a position inferior to that of uke.

This prolonged, sliding step, is a great asset in the sword arts, leading to a more extended range than uke expects. It can be used in many situations. When doing so, though, it is important not just to stretch the leg forward, but rather to push one's whole body ahead with the center, *tanden*, almost as if someone was actually pushing from behind one's back.

If you find it difficult to do this prolonged, sliding step, you are most certainly out of balance in one way or other. Even when having a stance where the feet are far apart, you should be able to slide forward several inches without any problem.

When doing so here, in movement four, make sure to let the right foot follow a bit, so that your right leg is out of the way of uke's sword, in case it would be coming all the way down to gedan. Also, twist the body in the taisabaki move, so that your shoulders are practically parallel to the direction of uke's sword, making sure to avoid it.

The position of tori's sword at the end of movement

four, horizontal and near tori's body, is to avoid it or the arm being struck by uke's sword. This position is reached by doing the *do* cut differently, slashing at the right side of uke's waist. Most of the cutting in this move is done by the sword being pulled back horizontally. In bokken practice with a part-

Aikibatto

ner, some contact is allowed and beneficial for learning the move – just be careful not to hit uke's ribs, which are rather fragile. Hitting the hip would not hurt uke, but is a bad aim – the *do* cut should be directed at the soft waist.

The vertical swinging of the sword in movement five, is done in such an angle as not to hit uke's sword. When it reaches *jodankamae* and the left hand grabs it, the edge of the sword should at once be directed at uke. At the same time, tori's body should turn toward uke, feet together, ready for the cut of movement six. That cut should follow immediately.

This cut should be regarded as an interrupted gedan cut, completed in slow motion at movement eight, when uke has backed off. If an actual *men* cut had been intended, the sixth movement way of doing it is still quite correct.

For a men cut, a high stance is to prefer, having the best chance of being above uke's guard, and also making a suitable angle for the cut. The short move of the men cut is actually more chopping than cutting, and that is the nature also of a deeper cut's first part – a chop which develops into a cut as the sword keeps on sliding down.

Movements eight to ten, the chiburi and noto, are the same as in hidari.

Iai considerations
In iai style solo training of the tori movements in this exercise, the modifications of the above would be: Some more extension and speed in the *do* cut of movement four, and the full *gedan* cut – no stop at head height – in movements six. The difference in extension and orb of the *do* cut is not that big at all from when done with a bokken on a partner. The blade just reaches a few more inches farther to the right, especially in the beginning of the cut.

Uke's movements in this exercise are not very meaningful to practice in a iai solo style.

5 Ukenagashi OMOTE

Starting position: Tori at right, uke at left.

1 Tori starts with bokken in belt, facing uke. Uke starts in chudankamae, sword drawn and held at middle guard, facing tori.

2 Uke steps forward with left foot, lifts sword to jodan-kamae, over the head.

3 Tori steps forward with left foot, drawing the sword. Uke steps forward with right foot.

4 Tori steps forward to the right with the right foot, and makes ukenagashi, parry on high level. Uke cuts chudan-giri, to middle level, in the direction of tori's original position.

5 Tori grips sword with both hands, while left foot goes to right foot, immediately followed by left foot taking half a step back, and kesagiri, diagonal cut, stopping above uke's neck.

Aikibatto

6 Uke yields sword to miginowaki, right side guard. Retreats three steps.

7 Tori pushes left foot further back and lowers the sword to gedan level, keeping it in a slightly diagonal track.

8 Chiburi migi, "shake off blood" to the right, by swinging the blade that way, then pulling it back to a position in front of the body, hilt to the left and sword tip to the right.

9 Noto, sword back into scabbard, by first swinging it downward 180°. Step back to the starting position.

Details

Aspects and considerations already treated in previous exercises of aikibatto are omitted here.

Ukenagashi is a most es-
sential parry, used in many
situations. In aikibatto shoden,
two exercises use it. They are
similar, except for the direction
taken by tori after the parry.

The ukenagashi should
not block the way of uke's
sword. The two blades need
not even touch - it is just an
additional precaution. In the
actual parry position, the
blade should be turned so that
the edge points slightly inward, a bit toward tori, so that
uke's sword, if touching tori's, will slide along the side, almost the back, of tori's sword. That way, no edge is damaged. Tori's sword should not be turned so much inward,
though, that the edge points at tori – for obvious reasons.

Furthermore, the sword should be held so high, that if
pushed toward tori by uke's sword, it would pass above the
head. Think of the sword as a sloping roof over your head.

It is important to draw the sword far out, when getting
it out of the scabbard, and then bring it back some in the
parry, so that the whole move has an elliptic track. If the
sword is not drawn in this extended way, part of it may still
be in the scabbard, when it is lifted. Also, the extension and
rounded return of the sword makes for better protection
than simply lifting the sword right up to parry.

Omote, straight, is the first of the two ukenagashi, the
other being *ura*, reverse. The pair of omote and ura, intensely
used in aikido, is much more than terms for the opposite
directions of approach. Originally the words refer to the inside and outside of clothing (the fur from an animal), and
they are full of implications. Omote is what is seen, ura the

hidden, omote is the direct and ura the indirect, and so forth.

These two principles are best expressed in aikibatto - and in aikido – if omote is done in a spirit of straightforwardness, whereas ura should be done with a measure of surprise, something totally unexpected and hard to comprehend for uke, even after the technique is completed. In omote, uke is immediately aware of what happened – although not having been able to stop it – but with ura, uke is almost mystified, confused. In aikido – and in these sword exercises – omote and ura are on a superficial level represented by stepping inside of uke's guard in the former, and outside of uke's guard in the latter.

The drawing of the sword in movement three prepares for the ukenagashi parry. The sword is pulled out in an extended move straight forward, with the hilt remaining in the front. The sword is then lifted upward and slightly back, into  the ukenagashi position, in movement four. The draw and the parry are done in one flowing move.

At the moment of the parry, tori's body is twisted sideways in *hanmi*, a slightly angular posture – not very much – and tori's left foot should have followed the right a bit, so as to avoid uke's blade completely, even at a *gedan* cut.

Immediately after the parry, tori puts the feet together, turns toward uke, grabs the sword with both hands, and does *kesagiri*, the diagonal cut, stopping above uke's neck. It is possible to do the cut very quickly after ukenagashi, if the parry is done correctly.

Kesagiri, the diagonal cut, has its name from a rude samurai joke: *Kesa* are the suspender straps worn by zen monks, crossing the chest in pretty much the direction that the cut is supposed to go.

The difference in angle between the straight cut and the diagonal kesagiri is not very big at all. The cut should go from uke's neck on one side and out by the waist, or not even exiting the body, on the other. This does not take as much of an angle as one might think.

The cut can be done in two different ways – one with the body leaning in a slightly diagonal way, the other with the body straight.

Cutting with the body straight would be best for the beginner, since it is important to establish the ability to always have a straight posture. This way of cutting can easily be applied in this exercise too. Then, the sword is not held at *jodankamae* right before the cut, but slightly to the side of the head, or even as far out as in *hassogamae*, the guard where the sword is held above the shoulder. The important thing is to hold the blade so that the edge is already directed exactly the way it will go in the cutting move – or one is sure to make an insufficient cut.

Cutting with a leaning body has got its points, too, once the student has learned a good posture. By leaning a little when doing kesagiri, the actual cut is, in relation to one's own body, exactly the same as the straight cut. This is the

Aikibatto

most powerful way of cutting, because of the symmetry of the body, and also has the benefit of sticking to the most important training in the sword arts – that of refining and perfecting the straight cut. The body leans ever so slightly, since the angle needed for the kesagiri is not very accentuated, and it is very important that one does not bend the body, but tilt it in a straight way – well, like the tower of Pisa.

When lowering the sword in movement seven, one keeps it going in the track it would follow if the kesagiri had been pulled through to *gedan* level. If the leaning way of cutting has been used, the body continues to lean with the same angle.

In this exercise, then, the body remains in the slightly tilted position until movement nine, when the sword tip enters the scabbard, which is turned so that the edge of the sword points upward. So, when the blade is adjusted into the position it will have when resting in the scabbard, that is the very moment when the body straightens.

The *chiburi* best used from this position, is where the sword is sort of whipped to the right, then pulled back to a position in front of tori, where the hilt is to the left and the sword tip to the right, just above tori's right knee. This should be an extended position, so that tori's arms are not bent but rather straight. Thereby, the sword is held at some distance from the body. It is a bit like presenting the blade to oneself. Actually, the position is intended for wiping off the sword properly with a cloth, before returning it to the scabbard.

The *noto* for this chiburi starts with the right hand reversing its grip on the hilt. Then the left hand lets go and the sword is allowed to swing, by gravity and no additional force, so that the tip of it goes downward from right to left side. There the sword is stopped, to be entered into the scabbard. As said above, if the leaning way of cutting kesagiri has been used, the body straightens up at the moment when the blade is turned so that its edge points upward. Note that when the blade is entered into the scabbard, the right hand grip on the hilt is pretty much the same as in *chiburi gedan* of hidari and migi.

Iai considerations

For *iai* style solo training of the tori movements in this exercise, the modification of the above would be: The *kesagiri* in movement five is not stopped at neck height, but pulled through to *gedan*.

Uke's movements in this exercise are not very meaningful to practice in a iai solo style.

6 Ukenagashi URA

裏

Starting position: Tori at right, uke at left.

1 Tori starts with bokken in belt, facing uke. Uke starts in chudankamae, sword drawn and held at middle guard, facing tori.

2 Uke steps forward with left foot, lifts sword to jodan-kamae, over the head.

3 Tori steps forward with left foot, draws the sword. Uke steps forward with right foot.

4 Tori steps forward to the right with the right foot, makes ukenagashi, parry on high level. Uke cuts men, to head level, in the direction of tori's original position.

5 Uke takes half a step back and lifts sword to jodan-kamae.

6 Tori steps with left foot forward to the left, on uke's right side, and grips sword with both hands. Right foot follows a bit, and the body turns sideways, facing uke.

7 Uke cuts chudangiri, to middle level, in the direction of tori's previous position.

8 Tori cuts kesagiri, diagonal, stopping above the neck on uke's right side.

9 Uke yields sword to miginowaki, right side guard. Retreats three steps.

10 Tori pushes right foot further back and lowers the sword to gedan level, keeping it in a slightly diagonal track. Turns the sword, so that the edge points straight down – and simultaneously straightens the body posture, if having done the leaning body kesagiri.

11 Tori steps back with left foot, and at the end of the step makes chiburi migi, "shake off blood" to the right, by swinging the blade that way, then pulling it back to a position in front of the body, hilt to the left and sword tip to the right.

12 Noto, sword back into scabbard, by first swinging it downward 180°. Step back to the starting position.

Aikibatto

Details

Aspects and considerations already treated in previous exercises of aikibatto, are omitted here. *Ukenagashi*, the high level parry, is commented in the text on omote. So are the basics of *omote* and *ura*, as well as *kesagiri*.

Ura, reverse, is the second of the two ukenagashi, differing from the first in movements five and on. Basically, the difference is that tori moves to the other side of uke after the ukenagashi parry, and the consequences thereof. Also, uke makes two charges instead of just one.

In movement five – because of having done the short *men* instead of the deeper *chudan* cut – uke is quick to draw for a new cut. Uke now takes aim at the point where tori stands after the ukenagashi parry.

Tori moves over to the right side of uke, getting very near uke by this move. There is no problem in this nearness, it is actually a common dueling distance in the old samurai arts. Since the actual cutting is done by pulling the sword back, starting very near uke only means that a lot more of the blade than just the outer part of it is involved in the cutting move. The step to the left with the left foot can be done immediately, but the body cannot follow until uke's sword is out of the way by being lifted to *jodankamae* – and then, there is need to hurry.

The kesagiri diagonal cut is from left to right, as opposed to right to left in omote, stopping above the right side of uke's neck. If tori uses the method of leaning with the body, it needs to be tilted to the left. In case of a straight body kesagiri, the sword should be held slightly to the left over the head – or left side *hassogamae*.

The straightening of the sword in movement ten is for a more pure and efficient chiburi at the next step. If the body is tilted from a leaning form of the kesa cut, this is the proper moment for adjusting the posture – or the backward step would be a bit awkward.

Chiburi in movement eleven is done the same way as in omote, except that it does not start from a standstill position, but begins just before the left foot backward step stops. From then on, it is the same as in omote.

Iai considerations

For *iai* style solo training of the tori movements in this exercise, the modification of the above would be: The kesagiri in movement eight is not stopped at neck height, but pulled through to gedan.

Uke's movements in this exercise are not very meaningful to practice in a iai solo style.

Aikibatto

7 Kote CHUDAN 中段

Starting position: Tori at right, uke at left.

1 Tori starts with bokken in belt, facing uke. Uke starts in miginowaki, side guard with sword drawn and held at right side.

2 Uke takes a big step forward, lifting sword to jodankamae, over the head.

3 Tori steps to the left with left foot, starts nukitsuke, the draw, slightly upward. Uke cuts chudangiri, to middle level, in the direction of tori's original position.

4 Tori takes right foot to left foot, twists the body to the left. Cuts kote, uke's right wrist at chudan level.

5 Tori turns the body toward uke, starts lifting the sword toward jodankamae, right foot forward to the left side of uke. Uke lifts sword to jodan-kamae, right foot backing to left foot.

6 Tori steps with left foot to right foot, turns the body toward uke. Uke cuts chudan-giri in the direction of tori's previous position.

9 Tori swings sword out to right side, at shoulder height, backing one step with right foot.

11 Noto, sword back into scabbard. Step back to the starting position.

7 Tori cuts yokomen, to the left side of uke's head.

8 Uke yields sword to miginowaki, right side guard. Retreats three steps.

10 Step back with left foot, chiburi jodan, "shake off blood" by swinging sword around in front of body.

Aikibatto

Details

Aspects and considerations already treated in previous exercises of aikibatto are omitted here.

Kote, wrist, is a sword technique aiming for that body part. In fencing, the wrist is often much easier to reach than the adversary's body, and certainly, by striking at the wrist, one still gets an essential advantage, making it infinitely more difficult for the attacker to move the sword sufficiently. If one wrist has been damaged, then the sword can be gripped by just one hand. For these two reasons, the kote technique is an important one in the Japanese sword arts.

Chudan, middle level, is the first of the two kote exercises, so named for hitting uke's wrist at middle level, when uke's position of the sword is pretty much identical to *chudankamae*, middle level guard – because of the previous *chudangiri*, cut to middle level.

This kote cut, executed immediately after the draw of the sword, is not far at all from the *nukitsuke*, the draw and strike, of mae and the other *shiho* exercises. The sword is drawn in much the same way, although coming down at the end instead of going forward horizontally in a *do* cut, and the body moves out of the way – although to the left instead of the right.

The most important difference is that of timing: In the shiho exercises, and many others as well, tori needs to get ahead of uke's cut, but in this one tori's sword needs not even be completely drawn until immediately after uke's cut. The best rhythm of the technique, though, is when tori's sword hits uke's wrist at the same time as uke's cut reaches its end.

Uke's starting position is different from every exercise preceding this one. It is *miginowaki*, right side guard, where the sword is held by the side of the body, its edge pointing to the right. The blade should either be completely horizontal, which feels a little stiff, or tipping slightly down backward, so that the point of it is lower than the hilt – not much, though, in a basic form of this guard.

Because of this position of the sword, the body is turned sideways, to make it possible for the left hand grip on the sword to be exactly in front of *tanden*, the center. Some prefer to keep the body straight, also in this guard, but I find that distinctly inferior. With the left hand directly in front of the center, or at least the vertical center line, one can move the sword the fastest and the strongest, since the left hand dominates when cutting with both hands gripping the sword.

When uke performs the cut of movements two and three, this is done by a big, flowing move without stop – from the side guard, over the head, and down to *chudan* level. This is a mighty cut that can still be done very quickly, when one learns to use one's body in the right way. The big cut is accompanied by a big step forward, where the right foot moves from behind to the front.

In the meantime, tori steps out to the left side, immediately starting to draw the sword in a slightly upward way, continuing in a circular move which finishes downward, onto uke's right wrist. Here, some contact is advantageous to learn the proper way of doing the technique. Usually, since uke's cut has the same direction as that of tori's kote cut, a slight contact should not hurt at all. Still, tori should be careful, not striking at a higher speed than can be controlled.

The kote position of the sword, when not cutting through, blocks uke's right hand. To raise it when tori's blade rests on it, would be unwise. Therefore, tori decides the moment when uke can draw the sword to *jodankamae* for the next cut. This is not done by moving the blade away, which would lack continuous control, but by changing the angle of it into a steep one, giving room for uke – just barely

– to raise the arms. This guiding move makes it pretty much compulsory for uke to do the jodankamae followed by a straight cut, which is in this case to the head, *men*, but could just as well be *chudan* or *gedan*, to middle or low level.

At the same time as tori opens for uke to raise the sword to jodankamae, tori takes a preparatory step with the right foot to the right. Do not wait with this step. When uke has reached the high guard position, the cut can follow very quickly indeed, and there will be no time for this  step. But when it has been taken beforehand, tori has to do little more than follow with the body, and slide along a bit with the left foot, to be out of the way of uke's cut.

Simultaneously, tori raises the sword in a semi-circle from its chudan position at the kote, to a jodankamae. From there, one could say that the second half of the circle is made in the *yokomen* cut to uke's left temple. The sword does not stop at *jodan*, but passes that position in its orbit from uke's right wrist to the left temple. This way, it's like the whole movement is one long yokomen cut.

The *chiburi jodan*, shaking off the blood at a high level, is well known in iaido – and not easy to do so that it feels comfortable. I find it ideal from a yokomen position, and that is precisely why it is used in this exercise.

Start by pulling the sword back from its yokomen extension, to a position where the sword tip points backward and the arm is stretched out to the side, at shoulder height. At the same time the right foot takes one full step back. The left hand goes to the left side, where the scabbard would be.

At this position, bend the

right arm at the elbow, so that the sword approaches the side of your head, but at the same time step back with the left foot.

Now, the sword hand should lead the sword to the position where your head was before backing one more step, and then continue in a big, circular move to the side, where the blade is tilted a bit forward, not so much, and the edge of the sword is to the right. Again, the right arm is extended to the right, at shoulder height.

This swinging the sword, which is the actual chiburi, should not be done by the whole arm, just the forearm, so that the elbow is the hub, the center of the circle. The best timing in this move, is when the sword reaches its right side position an instant after the left foot has finished its step.

Noto from this position is not very different from that in chiburi chudan, found in mae and ushiro. The right hand is lowered to middle level, at the same time as the sword is swung over to meet the scabbard, held by the left hand in front of *tanden*, the center. As the back of the blade slides on the left hand grip, the scabbard is moved along the side of

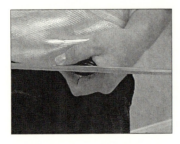 

Aikibatto

the body – very near it – so that you reach to get the sword tip into its opening. This movement should be done in a flowing way, not quick but with a steady pace.

When the blade enters the scabbard, or the belt if done with a bokken, the hilt should be straight ahead, neither to the right nor the left. Ideally *tsuba*, the sword guard, reaches the opening of the scabbard right in front of the center.

Iai considerations

For *iai* style solo training of the tori movements in this exercise, the modification of the above would really be just one: a proper extension of the yokomen cut. Also, certainly, the initial kote can be done in full speed, although not going any deeper than in partner training.

Uke's movements in this exercise are not very meaningful to practice in a iai solo style.

8 Kote JODAN

上段

Starting position: Tori at right, uke at left.
1 Tori starts with bokken in belt, facing uke. Uke starts in miginowaki, side guard with sword drawn and held at right side.

2 Uke takes a big step forward, lifting sword to jodankamae, over the head.

3 Tori steps to the right with right foot, left foot follows. Draws sword and cuts kote, uke's left wrist, from below, at jodan level. Uke starts a cutting move in the direction of tori's original position, but stops at left wrist's contact with tori's sword.

4 Tori lets the sword slide past uke's wrist, to a high position, continuing the cutting move.

5 Tori flips the sword around in the high position, so that the edge points at uke. Yokomen, cut to the left side of uke's head, with half a step back with left foot.

6 Uke yields sword to miginowaki, right side guard. Retreats three steps.

7 Tori swings sword out to right side, at shoulder height, backing one step with right foot.

8 Tori steps back with left foot, chiburi jodan, "shake off blood" by swinging sword around in front of body.

9 Noto, sword back into scabbard. Step back to the starting position.

Details

Aspects and considerations already treated in previous exercises of aikibatto are omitted here. *Kote*, wrist cut, is commented in the text on chudan. So is the *miginowaki* guard of uke, and the *chiburi* jodan.

Jodan, high level, or upper position, is the second of the two kote. Here, the wrist cut is done when uke charges with the sword raised high, right before uke's cut. This kote cut is one of the few fencing techniques described by Musashi in his *Book of Five Rings*. But the following up *yokomen* is an aikibatto addition.

Tori steps forward, starting to draw the sword, at the moment when uke begins the charge. There is no time to waste – the cut from *miginowaki* can be done faster than one would assume.

The timing of the kote, the cut to the wrist from below, is not that very tricky. The crux is to do it in a partner exercise without hurting uke. Some caution is needed, and it is preferable to practice it in slow motion, to establish a good understanding of it, before picking up speed.

Tori's bokken should touch uke's wrist, at the kote of movement three. In doing so, tori's sword grip should be firm enough almost to be able to halt the cut on its way. From below, the wrist is soft and therefore not too sensitive, but  of course some care is still called for. Also, the point of tori's bokken is not that far from uke's face, which is an additional reason for being careful.

The exact moment for the kote should be when uke's sword has started its downward move, and uke's hands are somewhere in front of uke's face. That is when the left wrist is the easiest to hit. That is also the moment when uke's arm is moving toward tori's sword, so that uke sort of helps in the kote cut. That exact moment might seem hard to find for tori, but is actually not so difficult – especially when doing the exercise a little faster. Still, use caution in the choice of speed, to avoid hurting uke.

At the kote hit, both tori and uke should stop their movement for a little while, to examine the position and balance, the stability of tori's sword grip, and so forth – but also in recognition of the fact that what comes next is a modification of the technique, in partner practice.

The kote would go right through uke's arm, in its original intent. This is modified into stopping when tori's bokken meets uke's wrist. Next, tori slides the bokken further on, upward to the right side, as if cutting through, and stops it in a high, extended position to the right. When tori's bokken has slid past uke's wrist, uke completes the *chudangiri* cut. This is to point out that the cut is not stopped by the kote technique.

At the same time as uke completes the cut, tori flips the extended sword by turning the right hand, so that the edge of the sword is directed at uke's left temple. Tori's left hand  grabs the hilt immediately thereafter. This flip of the sword can be quite awkward to do, needing some practice.

Speed as well as precision is essential. Once flipped, the sword should be in a correct position for the following *yokomen* cut, at uke's left temple, which is to be done as soon as tori's left hand has grabbed the sword. This tricky maneuver of movement five certainly takes time to learn, but will prove to be a very efficient technique, applicable in many situations.

An alternative solution for getting from the kote to the

yokomen, would be to continue the kote cut in a circularly swinging way, turning the hand at the end of it. Such a move, though, tends to make the previous kote cut imprecise. It is hard not to start turning the angle of the blade before the completion of that cut, making it pretty much useless.

The *chiburi* and *noto* are exactly the same as in chudan.

Iai considerations

For *iai* style solo training of the tori movements in this exercise, the modifications of the above would be two: The *kote* cut is not stopped, but pulled through to the high sword position, and the *yokomen* cut is extended instead of stopped short.

Uke's movements in this exercise are not very meaningful to practice in a iai solo style.

9 Harai ATE

当

Starting position: Tori at right, uke at left.

1 Tori starts with bokken in belt, facing uke. Uke starts in chudankamae, sword drawn and held at middle guard, facing tori.

2 Uke steps forward with left foot.

3 Tori steps forward to the right with right foot, firmly grabbing the scabbard and tsuba with left hand, and putting the right hand palm on hilt. Uke steps forward with right foot, and makes chudantsuki, thrust to middle level, in the direction of tori's original position.

4 Tori makes harai with tsuka, the hilt, in a semi-circular move from right to left, pushing uke's sword a bit to uke's right.

5 Tori turns body toward uke, makes tsukaate, strike at uke on chudan level with the hilt, and pushes uke backward. Uke falls back one full step with right foot, when pushed by tori, and draws sword to jodankamae.

7 Tori steps forward to the right with right foot, left foot following, cutting do, side cut on chudan level, with left hand helping to push the sword. Uke makes chudan-giri, cut to middle level.

6 Tori draws sword by pulling scabbard back, puts the left hand palm on the back of the blade, near its tip. Uke steps forward with right foot.

8 Tori raises the sword to jodankamae, left foot stepping to right foot, body turning toward uke. Cuts men, to the head.

9 Uke yields sword to miginowaki, right side guard. Retreats three steps.

10 Tori lowers sword to chudankamae, middle guard.

11 Chiburi kaiten, "shake off blood" by spinning the sword around.

12 Put blade on left shoulder. Noto, sword back into scabbard. Step back to the starting position.

Details

Aspects and considerations already treated in previous exercises of aikibatto are omitted here.

Harai, parry or warding off, sometimes pronounced *barai*, is a term used not only in the sword arts, but in some of the unarmed martial arts as well. It is neither a block nor only a parry, but a way of pushing uke's attack – either  ahead in line with uke's aim, or to the side, downward, or upward. By not only blocking uke's move, but giving it an additional impulse, it will take longer for uke to counter. Also, by such a move the options for uke's next attack can be limited.

Particularly in aikido style defense, the harai does not have much to do with avoiding uke's attack, since there is always a *taisabaki* move with the whole body for that purpose. Instead, the warding off movement is intended to direct uke into a particular move to do next, an impulse that uke should follow without thinking, if correctly applied.

Also, as mentioned above, the harai creates another rhythm, because of the slightly longer time it takes for uke to readjust for the next attack. The harai makes uke's initial attack prolonged beyond where uke has optimal balance and control – a bit like a push in the back of somebody walking by. There will be a stumbling, if only momentary, maybe only in the upper body. Still, that slows uke down somewhat.

In aikido too, the harai warding off is utilized in many techniques. Often, but not only, when uke attacks with strikes, such as *shomenuchi* or *tsuki*. Harai is also used when uke grabs for *gyakuhanmi katatedori*, but is warded off by tori's other hand before reaching the wrist. In *karatedo*, almost every block is harai, more or less in the same sense.

Ate, strike, is the first of the two harai. It is named after the punch at middle level done with *tsuka*, the hilt, in movement five. The warding off, done in the previous movement, gives uke a tendency to almost fall into the strike, which makes it more powerful. This striking with the hilt, *tsukaate*, is found in many a iaido kata – aiming either for the belly, as done here, or for the throat.

Uke is not cutting in the beginning of this exercise, but making *chudantsuki*, a thrust with the sword at middle level. This technique is done with quite a short forward move of the sword, or uke would be too much out of balance already before the harai. Also, uke's wrists would be too much exposed to a kote technique. Uke must be credited with a wiser behavior than that.

To reach with the tsuki, without stretching the arms too much forward, uke simply has to step in close before doing the thrust. Uke should have come so near, that the sword tip would almost touch tori's front, if tori remained on the spot. Then the tsuki thrust is only about a foot long – the equivalent of uke's body width from front to back.

Sometimes the blade is turned in tsuki, so that the edge points to the left or right instead of downward. This has practical reasons, relating to how to pierce a body, especially when wearing some kind of armour, or when hitting at the ribs. Here, though, the blade is kept at the same angle as in the original chudankamae – not that it would make any difference to tori.

The harai is best done right before uke's sword has come to a halt in the tsuki thrust. That is when it can break uke's balance the most. Tori swings the tsuka, the hilt, in a semi-circle from right to left side. Uke's sword is hit at the middle of this orb. That means the hit is pretty much in the

direction of uke's tsuki, but still making uke's sword fall off a little to uke's right. A well timed and focused harai can sometimes actually make uke drop the sword – especially if uke's sword grip needs improvement.

Tori needs to take care in doing the harai of movement four, since this is just about the only technique in the aikibatto shoden, where one might actually injure oneself, if doing wrong. The right hand cannot grip the hilt until after the warding off, or tori's fingers would smash uke's bokken. That hurts. Instead, the right hand is kept open, and the palm presses on the hilt, on the side away from where it hits uke's bokken.

The left hand, though, can and should grip the sword firmly – right where *tsuba*, the sword guard, would be. When done with a real sword, the left hand grip is on *saya*, the scabbard, right below the tsuba, and the thumb is on the tsuba, pressing the sword firmly into the scabbard. The sword should not be drawn even the least out of the scabbard, when harai is done.

At the ate strike, too, the sword is firmly held inside the scabbard. At that time, the right hand also has a firm grip, but on the hilt. A lot of the power in this strike comes from the body turn. In the harai move, tori has turned  sideways, and ate is done when turning back to face uke straight on.

The end of the hilt, *kashira*, hits uke in the belly – ideally in the solar plexus, but that should be avoided in partner practice. Still, there should be some contact between tori's bokken and uke's belly in this exercise, so as to learn correct timing, distance, and balance.

A good balance is also needed for pushing uke backward with an extension of the ate technique, in movement five. Normally, this extension of ate would be done without a pause, but then the partner is sure to feel discomfort, to say the least. Therefore, the ate move is stopped at a slight contact with uke's belly, and then continued in a push.

This pushing of uke is not only a way of learning proper extension of the ate technique, but also for the purpose of

creating enough room to draw the sword. When tori pushes uke back one full step, there is room between them for a safe draw.

The draw of the sword is done by sliding back left hand and turning the body to the left – not by extending the sword additionally forward, where uke might be able to reach and block it. With a real sword, the left hand draws back the scabbard, while the right hand keeps the sword in place.

As soon as the sword tip leaves the scabbard, the left hand gets behind it, starting to press the palm of the hand on the back of the sword. This is for support in the short and quick *do*, side cut, done next, when uke steps forward again for a second attack.

Uke's second attack is *chudangiri*, cut to middle level, but it might as well be *men* or *gedan*, making no difference to tori. If it is a *chudantsuki*, though, tori might find it difficult to sneak in with the sword under uke's guard, for the do cut. On the other hand, uke is not likely to choose the tsuki, since tori's sword is even more in the way, there at middle level. If uke were to try a *jodantsuki*, thrust on high level, tori should not have too much trouble finding room for the *do*.

The *do* cut is quickly followed by tori turning the body at uke's left side, simultaneously raising the sword to *jodan-kamae*. Then tori strikes with *men*, a cut to the head. The raising of the sword to the high level guard should be done to the position where tori will be at the end of the step in movement eight. This is much quicker than first raising the sword and then moving one's body.

The men cut is really intended to go down to chudan

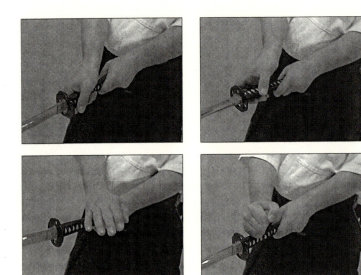

level, when not practicing with a partner. Here, though, the lowering of the sword to that position is done when uke has backed away. At the same time, left foot moves further back – as it would in an actual *chudangiri*, cut to middle level.

The *chiburi* here I call *kaiten*, rotating, because it involves a 360° spin of the sword around its own axis, counterclockwise. This way of chiburi is popular in some iaido schools. It takes time to learn – and in the meantime there is a great risk of dropping one's sword, which is as noisy as it is embarrassing. I recommend some practice at home.

The rotation of the sword is done by a push with the right hand. The hand should not move upward. That would risk throwing one's sword into one's own face. The hand moves diagonally to the left – as if wanting to hit one's own left upper arm. That way, the sword spins more steadily at the *chudankamae* position. There are other solutions for this chiburi, but this is the one I prefer.

The left hand grip at the end of the hilt, is fixed in its position in front of *tanden*, the center, but opening a little, for the sword to spin around inside of it. As soon as the sword has spun around one full 360°, the left hand grips it firmly

again. The right hand fist hits the hilt from above, as an additional chiburi move.

Also with the *noto* there are several ways of doing it. I prefer the way Nishio sensei taught, which seems to me to be the safe and controlled way of handling the sword. That is a most important aspect, since the blade is placed on the shoulder, right by one's own neck.

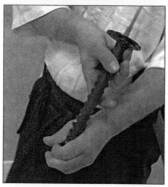

Start by tipping the sword up from the chudankamae position, to one where the back of the blade rests on the left shoulder. This is done by keeping the left hand grip in a fixed position in front of the center, while the right hand drags the sword up. It is a good precaution to make the edge of the blade point slightly to the left, away from the neck.

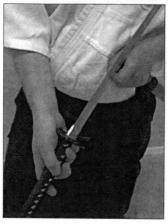

Next, release the right hand and grip the hilt anew, from below, with the thumb away from *tsuba*, the sword guard. Then the left hand grabs the scabbard, around its opening, and lifts it a bit toward the blade, which then slides on that grip until the sword tip can enter the scabbard.

Contrary to most other noto, when the blade has entered the scabbard completely, it is not the left foot stepping up to the right one, but the right foot steps back to the left – not that it is of immense significance, but still. The best harmony of the move, then, is to take this step in a sliding way at the same time as the blade enters the scabbard, and not after. Then the sword and the body both move backward.

Just as with other noto, the right hand finishes by sliding along the hilt to kashira, in this case on its underside.

Iai considerations
For *iai* style solo training of the tori movements in this exercise, the modifications of the above would be: A full thrust without any halfway stop in the *ate*, a proper extension of the *do* cut, and the *men* cut should go all the way down to *chudan* level.

Uke's movements in this exercise are not very meaningful to practice in a iai solo style.

10 Harai TSUKI

突

Starting position: Tori at left, uke at right.

1 Tori starts with bokken in belt, facing uke. Uke starts in chudankamae, sword drawn and held at middle guard, facing tori.

2 Uke steps forward with left foot.

3 Tori steps forward to the left with left foot, firmly grabbing the scabbard and tsuba with left hand, and putting the right hand palm on the hilt. Uke makes chudantsuki, thrust to middle level, in the direction of tori's original position.

4 Tori makes harai with tsuka, the hilt, in a semi-circular move from left to right, pushing uke's sword a bit to uke's left.

6 Uke steps forward with right foot.

5 Tori draws sword immediately after the harai, extending right arm to the right, sword held so that the edge points to the right. Uke steps back with right foot, and draws sword to jodankamae.

7 Tori makes chudantsuki, thrust to middle level, but places it by the right side of uke's waist. Uke cuts men, to the head, at tori's previous position.

8 Tori pushes uke back, by extending the tsuki thrust additionally, then pulls the sword back to a horizontal position near the body. Uke falls back one full step with right foot, when pushed by tori.

9 Uke yields sword to miginowaki, right side guard. Retreats two steps.

10 Tori steps back with left foot, while turning the sword so that the edge points to the floor, ending the step in a chudankamae position.

Aikibatto

11 Chiburi kaiten, "shake off blood" by spinning the sword around.

12 Put blade on left shoulder. Noto, sword back into scabbard. Step back to the starting position.

Details

Aspects and considerations already treated in previous exercises of aikibatto are omitted here. *Harai*, parry or warding off, is commented in the text on ate. So is *tsuki*, in general terms, and *chiburi kaiten*.

Tsuki, thrust, is the second of the two harai, named after the tsuki done by tori in movement seven. A significant difference to the previous harai exercise is that here, tori does a *taisabaki* move to the left instead of the right.

The harai in movement four is done similarly to the ate harai. Because tori is on the other side of uke, the semi-circular move is from left to right, pushing uke's sword slightly to uke's left.

Remember not to grip *tsuka*, the hilt, with the right hand until after harai is completed. Instead, keep the hand open, your palm on the side of the tsuka that is not hitting uke's sword. The left hand holds the scabbard, the thumb hooks *tsuba*, the sword guard, firmly. At the end of the harai, the sword is held horizontally.

The harai ends with a draw of the sword, tori's right hand pulling the sword horizontally to the right, left hand holding the scabbard back. It is very important not to start the draw already in the harai move, where the sword should be held very firmly inside the scabbard. When the draw commences, it is firstly done by the left hand thumb pushing the tsuba, so that the blade starts to slide out – and the rest of the draw is done by the right hand. When the sword is drawn, the edge of the blade points to tori's right.

After the sword is drawn, the blade is stabilized by its back being pressed against tori's body – still with the edge of the blade to the right, for obvious reasons. This is done not only to fix the position of the sword, but also to make sure that neither the sword nor the right arm is in the way of uke's following cut.

The *chudantsuki*, thrust to middle level, in movement

seven, is done with the blade still in the same position, its edge to the right. The tsuki is an unusually extended move, for two reasons: Uke has retreated after the harai, and since tori's next step is only a sliding forward to the left with the left foot, right foot following, uke can be hard to reach otherwise. Also, the tsuki will continue with the push of movement eight.

In partner training, the tsuki thrust is done at the right side of uke's waist, with a slight, sliding contact to uke's body. Make sure that the tip of your bokken does not hit uke at all! This is, of course, a modified version of an actual chudantsuki to the center of the body.

Pushing uke in the continued tsuki movement, is done to help get the sword back. That would take some effort, were the thrust an actual one with a real blade piercing uke's body. Directly after the push, tori pulls the sword back, to a horizontal position near the body, much like that of movement five. But this time, there is no contact between the blade and the body, nor is the right hand as far back as in movement five.

Now, tori steps back slowly with left foot, at the same time turning the blade clockwise, until the edge points to the floor and the sword is held in a normal chudan position. At the end of the step, the left hand approaches and grips the hilt, so that the step ends in a correct *chudankamae*, middle level guard position.

The *chiburi* is *kaiten*, the counterclockwise rotation of the sword described in the text on ate. The *noto*, too, is done exactly as in that exercise.

Iai considerations

For *iai* style solo training of the tori movements in this exercise, the modification of the above would be only one: A correct direction for the *chudantsuki* of movement seven – right at where uke would be.

Uke's movements in this exercise are not very meaningful to practice in a iai solo style.

Aikibatto Jo

Jo against sword exercises

Introduction

Aikibatto is primarily a system of sword exercises, but I have found the need for some *jo* exercises as well. The jo is a round staff with the standard length of 4.21 *shaku*, which is 127.5 centimeters (50 inches), and a diameter of around 25 millimeters (one inch). It is almost as commonly used in aikido training, as the ken is.

The techniques used vary significantly from dojo to dojo, and are often quite a handful to remember – even more so to handle diligently. The training of basic jo movements might be neglected, if there is a great volume of techniques needed to be memorized. That leads to an impressive amount of combinations, performed in a not so impressive way.

I do hope that this system does not add to that problem. Parallel to what is intended with the ken exercises of aikibatto, these jo counterparts are primarily meant as a sort of *suburi* - basic training of the basic movements with the jo.

The jo exercises are almost exact counterparts to the *ken* exercises, so that *mae* with the jo differs very little from *mae* with the ken, and so forth. The only alterations made, are those necessary because of the differences between the jo and the ken. These differences are big enough, for sure, but then again no bigger than that the sword moves can easily be transformed to jo ones, and vice versa.

Historically, the jo was used as a weapon against the sword. Of course, it is also possible to have paired exercises with jo against jo, but that would lead a bit too far away from the basic aikibatto concept to be meaningful – at least in the shoden set. We will see what might happen in the oku-den exercises, when they are completed.

Here, then, is the set of ten shoden exercises, with tori using a jo and uke a ken. Uke is actually doing exactly the same moves as in the ken exercises. For tori, there are some modifications, but not more than for the set to keep the same names as in the ken set – although that does in a few cases lead to some contradictions of terms.

One thing which sets the working with a jo apart from that of the ken, is that the former is so to speak ambidextrous. All jo movements can be done from the left as well as from the right. Even the very basic guard, which I simply call *chudankamae*, can be left sided as well as right sided. That would immediately double the number of exercises, easily creating the problem I mentioned above, about too many combinations taking the focus from the training of the basic movements.

So, I stick to a one sided handling of the jo, beginning with the guard which relates directly to the sword guard. That is with the jo on the left side in chudankamae. Then tori has got the right foot and right hand forward, just like in the chudankamae for the sword. For basic exercises, this makes the most sense.

The adventurous student should feel free to try the exercises also with a start from the right sided chudankamae. Then all the following moves should be done on opposite sides to what is shown here. I do not recommend this, before familiarizing properly with the exercises as they are presented.

Aikibatto

Muso Gonnosuke Katsuyoshi was a samurai in the early 17ᵗʰ century Japan, who founded the jodo school Shinto Muso ryu. According to legend, he had been skilled with the bo, among other weapons, but shortened it to jo length after being defeated by Musashi in a duel. At their next encounter, he used the jo against Musashi. Sources differ as to how the second duel ended – either a draw, or victory for Gonnosuke.

Jo basics

Regarding basic elements of jo, such as how to grip it, how to do tsuki, uchi and so forth, there is almost as much to be said as about the sword. And just as with the sword, the best way to learn it is to be aware of the jo as a tool, and how to utilize it optimally in relation to its own design and functionality. If you keep that in mind, then you are unlikely to go wrong.

For example, the sword cuts, but the jo does not. Any movement with either one must be done in full awareness of this. Also, the jo has two identical ends, whereas on the sword they differ tremendously. Think about it – the consequences are decisive on how to move the sword or the jo.

Depending on what tool is used, the ken or the jo, one would also naturally adjust the movements of one's body. Armed with the sword, you move forward more boldly and directly, making evasive steps no more to the side than what is absolutely necessary, and so forth. With the jo, though, all movements are more evasive, and with additional margin, since the jo needs some room to be used powerfully, but the sword cuts severely even when not swung with great force.

I think it is safe to say that the sword is the mightier weapon of the two. But that does not mean the jo is futile. This, the legend has it, was proven by its inventor Gonno-

Yokomen with jo, and with ken.

suke in a duel against the mighty Miyamoto Musashi, which ended in a draw. But it is essential to respect the difference and make ones moves accordingly.

There are actually many similarities, as well. You should have the same straight posture whether you hold a jo or a ken, and you apply a very similar grip.

In your strikes with the jo, your grip should be done mainly with the little fingers, and your hands should be turned inward, similarly to the ken grip. By this grip, the jo is effectively supported by your arms, and your wrists are firm. That gives stability to the strikes.

You must use your center, *tanden*. This is as true with the jo as it is with the ken. A powerful *tsuki* thrust is with your rear hand not going far-ther than to your center. In any *uchi*, the hand closest to your body should feel linked to your center. Make sure that your center is directed toward the target, whatever strike you do.

In *tsuki*, naturally, it is with the end of the jo that you strike. This is also true for *uchi*, the circular strikes. You should hit with the edge of the jo's end, and not the side of it. That

Aikibatto

is the hardest part of the jo. Also, the striking area is the smallest possible, which increases the effect of it.

You must be aware of the differing targets for the jo and the ken. The sword pierces and cuts, whereas the jo can only hit. They must be used accordingly. The jo has much fewer targets than the ken does. For *tsuki*, the thrust, there are basically three targets: *men* for the throat or head, *chudan* for solar plexus, and *gedan* for the knees. The *uchi* strike can be done to the side of the head, *yokomen*, to the wrist, *kote*, although that is little more  than a blocking technique, and *gedan*, to the knee. Other striking targets are either quite ineffective or far from basic.

You need more power in strikes with the jo, than you do with the sword. The jo can only hit, not cut or pierce, so you have to be able to hit hard enough. This is true for tsuki as well as uchi. Actually, if you move and use your body more in line with what boxers do, you will find the way to gain power in your strikes.

Of course the wooden jo is weaker than the steel of the sword blade, so one should avoid head on strikes between the two. Still, the jo is not as weak as one might think. Not even at right angle is it that easy to cut through with a sword, so with any other angle the blade is more likely to be warded off. Nonetheless, one should make sure to have the jo meet the sword in angles as far away from 90° as possible, to avoid the risk of getting the jo damaged.

The movements you make when you have the jo, have more of *taisabaki* in them, than what is common in swordplay. You move from side to side, avoiding as much as possible to face the attacker straight on. In this way, jo techniques are quite similar to aikido.

Enough said, let's go to the exercises and examine the matter further by practicing.

Jo exercises

Shoden 初伝

SHIHO four directions 四方

1   MAE front 前

2   USHIRO back 後

3   HIDARI left 左

4   MIGI right 右

UKENAGASHI parry 受流

5   OMOTE straight 表

6   URA reverse 裏

KOTE wrist 小手

7   CHUDAN middle 中段

8   JODAN high 上段

HARAI ward off 払

9   ATE strike 当

10   TSUKI thrust 突

Tori: Stefan Stenudd. Uke: Tomas Ohlsson.

       Aikibatto

1 Shiho MAE

Starting position. Tori at left, uke at right.

1 Tori starts with jo by left side, facing uke, feet together. Uke starts in chudankamae, sword drawn and held at middle guard, facing tori.

2 Uke steps forward with left foot, lifts sword to jodankamae, over the head.

3 Tori steps forward with left foot, jo to chudankamae, middle guard.

4 Uke steps forward with right foot. Tori steps forward to the right with the right foot, makes gedanuchi, low level hit on uke's knee, while uke's arms are still raised.

5 Uke makes chudangiri, vertical cut to middle level, in the direction of tori's original position.

6 Tori lifts jo to jodankamae, over the head, and turns toward uke.

7 Tori makes yokomen uchi, hit to the side of uke's head.

8 Uke yields sword to miginowaki, right side guard. Retreats three steps.

9 Tori pulls jo back to chudankamae, middle guard. Steps back to the starting position.

Ending position. Tori at left, uke at right.

2 Shiho USHIRO

Starting position. Tori at left, uke at right.

1 Tori starts with jo at left side, back turned to uke. Uke starts in chudankamae, sword drawn and held at middle guard, behind tori.

2 Uke steps forward with left foot, lifts sword to jodan-kamae, over the head.

3 Tori steps forward with left foot, then right foot forward to the right. Uke steps forward with right foot.

4 Uke makes chudangiri, cut to middle level, in the direction of tori's previous position.

5 Tori turns around on the spot, then takes the jo to chudankamae. Uke takes a short step back, draws sword to jodankamae, and steps forward with the right foot.

6 Tori steps forward to the right with the right foot, makes gedanuchi, low level hit on uke's knee, while uke's arms are still raised.

7 Uke makes chudangiri, cut to middle level, in the direction of tori's former position.

8 Tori lifts jo to jodankamae, over the head, and turns toward uke. Yokomen, hit to the side of uke's head.

9 Uke yields sword to miginowaki, right side guard. Retreats three steps.

10 Tori pulls jo back to chudankamae, middle guard. Steps back to the starting position.

Aikibatto

3 Shiho HIDARI

Starting position. Tori at left, uke at right.

1 Tori starts with jo by left side, uke on forward left. Uke starts in chudankamae, sword drawn and held at middle guard, tori on forward right.

2 Tori steps forward with left foot, then right foot, into front of uke.

4 Tori steps forward to the right with the right foot, makes gedanuchi, low level hit on uke's knee, while uke's arms are still raised.

3 Tori turns toward uke, left foot forward, jo to chudankamae, middle guard. Uke steps forward with left foot, lifts sword to jodankamae, over the head.

5 Uke makes chudangiri, vertical cut to middle level, in the direction of tori's original position.

6 Tori lifts jo to jodankamae, over the head, and turns toward uke. Yokomenuchi, hit to the side of uke's head.

7 Uke yields sword to miginowaki, right side guard. Retreats three steps.

8 Tori pulls jo back to chudankamae, middle guard. Steps back.

4 Shiho MIGI 右

Starting position. Tori at right, uke at left.

1 Tori starts with jo by left side, uke on forward right. Uke starts in chudankamae, sword drawn and held at middle guard, tori on forward left.

2 Tori steps forward with right foot, into front of uke.

3 Tori turns right foot and body toward uke, steps with left foot forward, jo to chudankamae, middle guard. Uke steps forward with left foot, lifts sword to jodan-kamae, over the head.

4 Uke steps forward with right foot. Tori slides further forward and to the left with the left foot, makes gedan-uchi, low level hit on uke's knee, tori's body twisting sideways. Uke makes chudan-giri, cut to middle level, in the direction of tori's previous position.

5 Tori swings the jo around in a vertical circle up to jodankamae.

6 Immediately after jodan-kamae, tori makes yokomen-uchi, hit to the side of uke's head.

7 Uke yields sword to miginowaki, right side guard. Retreats three steps.

8 Tori pulls jo back to chudankamae, middle guard. Steps back.

Ending position.

5 Ukenagashi OMOTE

Starting position. Tori at right, uke at left.

1 Tori starts with jo by left side, facing uke. Uke starts in chudankamae, sword drawn and held at middle guard, facing tori.

2 Uke steps forward with left foot, lifts sword to jodan-kamae, over the head.

3 Tori steps forward with left foot, jo to chudankamae, middle guard. Uke steps forward with right foot.

4 Tori steps forward to the right with the right foot, makes ukenagashi, parry on high level. Uke makes chudangiri, cut to middle level in the direction of tori's previous position.

5 Tori continues the movement of the jo, changing hands, passing jodankamae as with a sword, to yokomenuchi, hit to the side of uke's head.

6 Uke yields sword to miginowaki, right side guard. Retreats three steps.

7 Tori pulls jo back to chudankamae, middle guard. Steps back to the starting position.

Aikibatto

6 Ukenagashi URA

Starting position. Tori at left, uke at right.

1 Tori starts with jo by left side, facing uke. Uke starts in chudankamae, sword drawn and held at middle guard, facing tori.

2 Uke steps forward with left foot, lifts sword to jodan-kamae, over the head.

3 Tori steps forward with left foot, jo to chudankamae, middle guard. Uke steps forward with right foot.

4 Tori steps forward to the right with the right foot, makes ukenagashi, parry on high level. Uke cuts men, to head level, in the direction of tori's previous position.

5 Uke takes half a step back and lifts sword to jodan-kamae.

6 Tori follows immediately with jo, to press down on uke's wrist, left foot stepping forward to the left.

7 Tori pulls back the jo, turning the body to the sida, following with the right foot.

8 Uke makes chudangiri, cut to middle level in the direction of tori's previous position.

9 Tori turns the jo over, makes yokomenuchi, hit to the side of uke's head.

10 Uke yields sword to miginowaki, right side guard. Retreats three steps.

11 Tori pulls jo back to chudankamae, middle guard. Steps back to the starting position.

　　　　　　　　　　　　Aikibatto

7 Kote CHUDAN 中段

Starting position. Tori at left, uke at right.

1 Tori starts with jo by left side, facing uke. Uke starts in miginowaki, side guard with sword drawn and held at right side.

2 Uke takes a big step forward, lifting sword to jodankamae, over the head.

3 Tori steps forward to the left with left foot, jo to chudankamae, middle guard. Follows with right foot.

4 Uke cuts chudangiri, to middle level, in the direction of tori's previous position.

5 Tori twists the body, makes kote, strike at uke's wrist from above.

6 Tori releases uke by lifting the front end of the jo, followed by the right foot stepping to the right.

7 Uke draws the sword to jodankamae, backing half a step, and cuts in the direction of tori's previous position.

8 Tori makes yokomenuchi, strike to the left side of uke's head.

9 Uke yields sword to miginowaki, right side guard. Retreats three steps.

10 Tori pulls jo back to chudankamae, middle guard. Steps back to the starting position.

Aikibatto

8 Kote JODAN 上段

2 Uke takes a big step forward, lifting sword to jodankamae, over the head.

4 Tori slides down to forward end of jo with the left hand grip, and reverses the right hand grip.

Starting position. Tori at left, uke at right.
1 Tori starts with jo by left side, facing uke. Uke starts in miginowaki, side guard with sword drawn and held at right side.

3 Tori steps forward with left foot, jo to chudankame. Immediately tori takes next step with right foot forward to the right, swings jo up to uke's throat and chin. Uke starts a cutting move, but stops when tori's jo reaches the chin.

5 Tori turns body slightly counter-clockwise and lets left foot follow. Yokomenuchi, strike to the left side of uke's head. Uke continues the cutting move, once tori's jo moves away from the chin.

6 Uke yields sword to miginowaki, right side guard. Retreats three steps.

7 Tori pulls jo back to chudankamae, middle guard. Steps back to the starting position.

9 Harai ATE

Starting position. Tori at left, uke at right.

1 Tori starts with jo by left side, facing uke. Uke starts in chudankamae, sword drawn and held at middle guard, facing tori.

2 Uke steps forward with left foot.

3 Tori steps forward to the right with right foot, turns jo over to the right, grabs with both hands. Uke steps forward with right foot, makes chudantsuki, thrust to middle level, in the direction of tori's previous position.

4 Tori makes harai with the jo, in a semi-circular move from right to left, pushing uke's sword a bit to uke's right.

5 Tori continues jo movement, moves left hand to grip left end of jo. Uke draws sword to jodankamae.

6 Tori makes chudantsuki, strike at middle level, pushing uke back.

9 Tori draws jo up to jodan-kamae. Turns right hand grip on jo.

11 Uke yields sword to miginowaki, right side guard. Retreats three steps.

12 Tori pulls jo back to chudankamae, middle guard. Steps back to the starting position.

7 Uke falls back one full step with right foot, when pushed by tori, and keeps sword in jodankamae.

8 Tori pulls jo slightly back, opens the left hand grip to slide on the jo. Steps to the right with right foot, left foot following. Makes gedanuchi, hit to the knee. Uke steps forward with right foot, and cuts chudangiri, to middle level.

10 Tori turns body toward uke, left foot following. Yokomenuchi, strike to the left side of uke's head.

Aikibatto

10 Harai TSUKI

Starting position. Tori at left, uke at right.

1 Tori starts with jo by left side, facing uke. Uke starts in chudankamae, sword drawn and held at middle guard, facing tori.

2 Uke steps forward with left foot.

3 Tori steps forward to the left with left foot, turns the jo up, puts right hand above the left hand grip.

4 Uke makes chudantsuki, thrust to middle level, in the direction of tori's previous position.

5 Tori makes harai with the jo, in a semi-circular move from left to right, pushing uke's sword a bit to uke's left.

6 Tori slides with right hand and grips the right side end of the jo, then slides with left hand to grip the other end of the jo. Uke steps back with right foot, and draws sword to jodankamae.

7 Uke steps forward with right foot.

8 Tori makes chudantsuki, thrust to middle level, and pushes uke backward. Uke cuts men, to the head, in the direction of tori's previous position. Uke retreats one step with right foot when pushed.

9 Tori draws jo to jodan-kamae, stepping in with right foot. Uke yields sword to miginowaki, right side guard. Retreats two steps.

10 Tori pulls jo back to chudankamae, middle guard. Steps back to the starting position.

Glossary

Sword techniques

kamae guard
jodankamae high guard
chudankamae middle guard
gedankamae low guard
hassogamae shoulder guard
miginowaki right side guard
hidarinowaki left side guard
hanmigamae angled guard

batto drawn sword
nukitsuke sword draw and strike in one move
ukenagashi parry
harai ward off
katate one-handed
morote two-handed

ate strike
gamenate head strike
chudanate middle level strike

tsuki thrust
jodantsuki high level thrust
chudantsuki middle level thrust

kote wrist cut
do trunk cut (*yokogiri*)

kiri (*giri*) cut
jodangiri cut to high level (*men*)
chudangiri cut to middle level

gedangiri cut to low level
men head cut
shomen straight head cut
yokomen side head cut
kesagiri diagonal cut
yokogiri horizontal cut (*do*)
shihogiri cutting in four directions
happogiri cutting in eight directions
tameshigiri test cutting
chiburi shake off blod
noto sheathe the sword

Sword parts

boshi pattern on swordtip
fuchi metal sleeve on hilt
habaki metal collar on blade
hamon pattern on blade
ji blade surface
jigane between *hamon* and *shinogi*
kashira hilt pommel
kissaki point section
kojiri scabbard butt cap
ko-shinogi ridgeline
kurigata knob on scabbard
mekugi-ana peg hole
menuki hilt ornament
mune back of blade
nakago tang
sageo cord on scabbard
saya scabbard
shinogi ridgeline
shinogi-ji between *shinogi* and *mune*
tsuba sword guard
tsuka hilt
yakiba tempered line
yokote ridgeline behind point

Aikibatto

Swords

ken sword (double edged)
katana long sword
to sword
daito long sword
tachi sword (reverse mounting)
kodachi small *tachi*
wakizashi short sword
tanto knife (*tanken*)
kozuka small knife on scabbard
iaito training sword
bokken wooden sword
bokuto wooden sword
shinai kendo sword of bamboo
daisho pair of swords

Counting

1	**ichi**
2	**ni**
3	**san**
4	**shi** (*yon*)
5	**go**
6	**roku**
7	**shichi** (*nana*)
8	**hachi**
9	**ku**
10	**ju**
11	**ju-ichi**
	...
20	**ni-ju**
21	**ni-ju-ichi**
	...
100	**hyaku**
1000	**sen**

General

Dojo
do (*michi*) way
dojo training hall
shomen head side
kamiza honorary seat
shinzen the gods
tatami mat

People
shoshinsha beginner
uchideshi boarding student
kohai junior student
sempai senior student
sensei teacher
kyu beginner's grade (5-1)
dan advanced grade (1-10)
mudansha without dan grade
yudansha with dan grade
fukushidoin assistant instructor
shidoin instructor
shihan advanced instructor
renshi 4-6 dan
kyoshi 6-7 dan
hanshi 8 dan -

Garment
dogi training gear
keikogi training gear
obi belt
hakama wide trousers

Training
keiko (*geiko*) training
keikosha training person, trainee
rei bow

shomen rei bow to head side
otagai ni rei mutual bow
to rei bow to sword
za rei seated bow
ritsu rei standing bow
reigi etiquette
onegai shimasu please
arigato gozaimasu thank you very much
dozo go ahead
hai yes
iie no
hajime start
yame stop
osame end
kata formal training
randori free training
jiyuwaza free training
suburi basic exercises
maai correct distance
taisabaki body move
misogi purification
mokuso (*zazen*) meditation
shiai competition
kumite competition
ippon one point
dame bad
shui warning
Directions
jodan high level
chudan middle level
gedan low level
mae forward
ushiro behind
migi right
hidari left
shiho four directions
happo eight directions

Attitude
shisei posture
shizentai natural posture
hara belly
harakiri cutting belly
seppuku cutting belly
kokoro heart
shin heart, spirit
zanshin extended spirit
kokyu breath
kokyuryoku power breath
ki life energy
kiai joint energy, shout
kime focusing
koshi hip
tanden center
ku (*kara*) emptiness
in yin
yo yang

Other
ai joining
aiki joining life energy
aikido the way of joining life energy
aikidoka aikido practitioner on a professional level
Aikikai aikido organization (*Zaidan Hojin Aikikai*)
bu war
budo the way of war
budoka budo practitioner on a professional level
bushi warrior
bushido the way of the warrior
Go rin no sho Book of Five Rings, by Miyamoto Musashi
iai joining with being, alertness
iaido sword art
jo staff 127 centimeters
jodo the way of the staff
ju soft
judo the way of softness

jujutsu the art of softness
jutsu technique, art
kai organization
ken sword
kendo the way of the sword, fencing
kobudo old budo
koryu old school
okuden inner mediation
ronin masterless knight
ryu ryu
samurai knight
shoden first mediation
Zen Nippon Kendo Renmei (ZNKR) All-Japan Kendo Federation

Aikibatto

Shoden
SHIHO four directions
1   MAE front
2   USHIRO back
3   HIDARI left
4   MIGI right
UKENAGASHI parry
5   OMOTE straight
6   URA reverse
KOTE wrist
7   CHUDAN middle
8   JODAN high
HARAI ward off
9   ATE strike
10   TSUKI thrust

Okuden
NAGARE flowing
TANINZUGAKE several attackers

Breinigsville, PA USA
19 January 2010
231012BV00001B/171/P